The Contact Cosmogram

Reinhold Ebertin

ISBN-10: 0-86690-088-8
ISBN-13: 978-0-86690-088-1

Cover Design: Jack Cipolla
Translation: Linda Kratzsch

Published by:
American Federation of Astrologers, Inc.
6535 S. Rural Road
Tempe, AZ 85283

www.astrologers.com

Printed in the United States of America

Contents

Dedication

To my dear wife

Chapter One

The Contact Cosmogram

Everyone is born into a very particular kind of environment, and from birth his or her relationship to mother, father, siblings, relatives, and neighbors is a very definite one. In the course of time, special relationships will develop with friends, teachers, superiors, and colleagues. The people with whom the individual comes into more or less close contact vary greatly. Nevertheless, the kind of relationship existing in each case can be determined by means of the natal aspects or the cosmograms. Disease and character can be inherited, as can the probability of a mutual attraction or suffering caused by another person. Even the relationship between murderer and victim can be read in the contact cosmogram.

The practice of comparing the horoscopes of two individuals has long been the custom in traditional astrology. Its purpose is to determine whether any permanent harmony or lasting happiness in love or marriage could result. In the light of modern experience, various errors were made in these comparisons. In the first place, the orb taken for the mutual aspects was much too great. Also, the belief was that the trine aspect was favorable (a special kind of harmony is presumed to exist with this aspect), and likewise there is the belief that certain disadvantages are inherent in the hard aspects (square, opposition, etc.). Today we know it is not the kind of aspect but the nature of the heavenly bodies that must be used as the basis for comparison.

In my book *The Cosmic Marriage* I explain that it is not the similarity but rather the mutual complement as shown by the cosmograms that is of significance. If for instance a trine is used as a basis, then signs of the zodiac that are similar in character (choleric, sanguine, melancholy, phlegmatic) can be compared. For example, neither two aggressive natures nor two truly phlegmatic types are suited to uphold any lasting good relationship.

The comparison of horoscopes in astrology was primarily concerned with the love life. But I prefer the term "contact cosmogram" to the word "horoscope" because the former is much more versatile and comprehensive in scope.

Our lives are subject to constant change. Human relationships also fluctuate and change. So, no solid groundwork exists for the comparison of cosmic birth charts; rather, one must realize that here, too, changes will come about. A love relationship that at the onset seems happy and full of promise will go through many crises that can be overcome but which are just as liable to bring the relationship to an end. If for example a harmonious aspect is transited by a slow-moving body (Saturn, Uranus, Neptune), the mutual relationship can expect hard trials ahead.

The obvious conclusion to be drawn from this is that the mutual aspects have to be limited as far as possible to one or two degrees. Otherwise the joint stimulation of a constellation in the good or bad sense just isn't possible.

The contact cosmogram is primarily concerned with the stellar positions at the time of birth and is studied in relationship to current conditions. The basis of calculation is the 90° circle, and the signs of the zodiac are arranged in the circle as follows: Aries, Cancer, Libra, Capricorn (0-30°), Taurus, Leo, Scorpio, Aquarius (30-60°), and Gemini, Virgo, Sagittarius, Pisces (60-90°). In this way, the conjunctions, squares and oppositions of the individual factors all coincide, while the 45° and 135° aspects are located opposite one another.

Setting Up the Contact Cosmogram

Prerequisites of a contact cosmogram are two computed natal chars. In addition, it is important to check the Midheaven and Ascendant in relationship to events in life to be sure of their accuracy. If the time of birth is unknown, one can use the noon positions, although the inclusion of the Midheaven and Ascendant is preferred. But a natal chart without the birth time is better than none at all since valuable information can still to be gleaned. For reasons of discretion, birth data is not always included in the examples.

In order to orientate yourself with the 90° circle, please look at Figure 1. The inner zodiacal circle and the outer 90° circle are to be

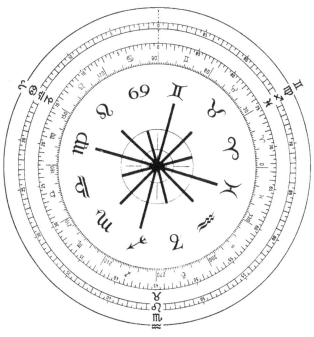

Figure 1

3

considered as completely separate entities. Hence any planet located in the inner circle has no connection whatsoever with any planet found at the same corresponding position in the 90° circle. To demonstrate this more clearly, let us look at Manfred's natal chart (see Figure 2). Here, the Sun is located at 3 Aries 38 and should therefore also be located in the 90o circle, in the upper left sector, at 3°38'. Uranus at 18°25' also must be transposed in the same manner. Pluto at 19 Cancer 58 and the Moon at 28 Libra 08 are likewise entered in this sector.

The factors in the signs of Taurus, Leo, Scorpio, and Aquarius are entered between 30 and 60 degrees. Accordingly, Saturn is located at 2 Aquarius 41, or 32°41', and the Midheaven at 6 Aquarius 06 below, or at 36°06'. The factors in the signs of Gemini, Virgo, Sagittarius, and Pisces come into the upper sector between

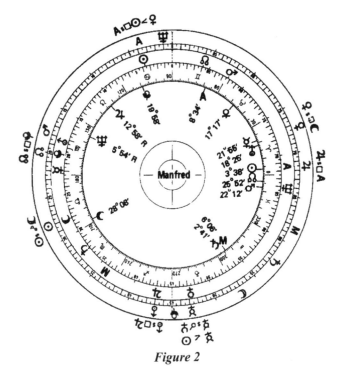

Figure 2

60 and 90 degrees (0°). Thus, Neptune is at 5 Virgo 54 Virgo, or 65°54'.

There are no houses in the contact cosmogram as the only deciding factors are the planets, Midheaven and Ascendant in their reciprocal relationships. The heavenly bodies can form angles or aspects to one another: Mercury and Pluto form a square aspect (90°), so in the 90° circle we see them close together. Saturn and the Midheaven form a conjunction. It is not necessary to calculate the aspects because they are immediately identifiable in the 90o circle.

The midpoints are a special kind of aspect in which one factor is located in the middle between two other factors. This can be clearly seen in the case of Pluto between Mercury and Uranus in the 90° circle. In the inner 360° circle we find the Pluto square be-

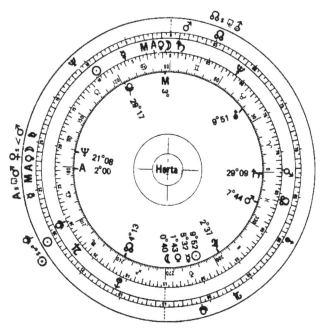

Figure 3

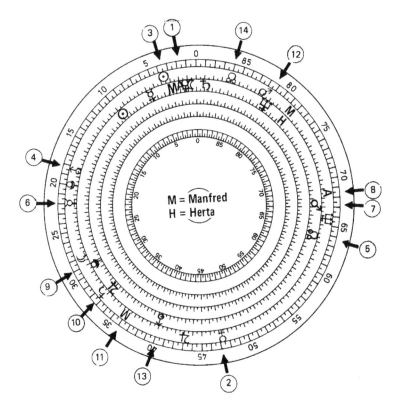

Figure 4

tween Mercury and Uranus. The notation is then: Pluto = Mercury/Uranus. Equally as obvious is Saturn's position in the 90° circle between the Moon and Midheaven (Saturn = Moon/MC). This constellation is difficult to recognize in the inner circle. The semisquare of Saturn is at 17 Sagittarius 41, and this point lies in the middle between the Moon and Midheaven.

The outer ring contains those points progressed by the solar arc and which apply to the couple's wedding day.

After studying Herta's cosmogram (see Figure 3), we set up the contact cosmogram for both partners (see Figure 4). The positions

6

of the man are entered in the outer ring and the woman's positions in the next ring toward the inside. Notice the series of points at which factors of both partners coincide; these points are marked by numbers in little circles. The investigation is best carried out using the 90o workboard or the familiar 90° calculating disc because in order to determine the 45° and 135° angles we have to refer to the corresponding opposite points in the 90° circle. At (1) and (2) we see that the Venus positions of both partners are exactly opposite one another. This is especially conducive to a strong attraction. Now taking a look at the partners' charts, we find the Venus positions semisquare (135°) to one another. This is sufficient for a first interpretation. It is important to refer to the individual natal charts as well as the contact cosmogram.

At (3), Manfred's Sun and Herta's Midheaven coincide. This indicates a very deep, personal relationship between the two people. If the orb is increased somewhat, we find that Manfred's Sun aspects Herta's Moon, Venus, Ascendant, and Midheaven. This is enough to tell us there is a close bond between the two that is liable to lead to an intimate relationship, if not to marriage.

At (4) and (5), Manfred's Uranus and Moon's Node ware mutually aspected. This leads to the conclusion that the relationship is one that came about suddenly (Uranus) or one full of tension (Uranus). In close proximity (6), Manfred's Mercury and Herta's Mars (7) point to conflict (Mars) and discussion (Mercury). These features could eventually undermine the relationship because Manfred's Neptune (7) is situated between Herta's Mars and the Moon's Node. At (8), the Ascendant aspecting Herta's Mars is an additional indication of conflict and altercation. At (9), Manfred's Moon and Herta's Pluto are in mutual aspect, which can indicate a fateful relationship. One could perhaps even say that the husband could experience severe emotional shocks related to Herta's Pluto.

At (10), Saturn and Jupiter, suffering and joy, come together. The Midheaven at (11) is located opposite Manfred's Mars and Herta's Neptune (12), which can indicate a weakening (Neptune of the male's willpower (Mars = Manfred's Midheaven). At (13) and (14) we find the reverse of (4) and (5), and the disturbing factor of Uranus, which threatens to destroy the uniting element, the Moon's Node.

One principle must be clearly stated: there is no such thing as a stable and fixed cosmogram. Rather, each and every cosmic constellation, due to the motion of the transits and directions, is subject to change. It is a complete fallacy to assume that a few good aspects in the contact cosmogram mean permanent harmony.

The Contact Cosmogram Is Subject to Change

Let us first take a look at the directions, which in this case correspond in both natal charts to the couple's marriage. The positions progressed by solar arc can be found in Figure 2 in the outermost ring. In Manfred's case, the solar arc Ascendant meets Sun and Pluto and signifies a fateful association. Theosophists and members of the Rose and Cross Society would in this case speak of a"karmic bond. At the same time, there is also a correlation to the female Moon's Node in the contact cosmogram at (5).

Solar arc Sun aspecting the natal Moon is a typical marriage constellation, which coincides here with Herta's Pluto. We find repeatedly that the mutual constellations in the contact cosmogram are also triggered by directions. Solar arc Uranus over Jupiter is indicative of some sudden change in life, at times also of sudden (Uranus) happiness or good fortune (Jupiter). However, we must not overlook the fact that Herta's Saturn is located in the contact cosmogram at the spot opposite. Solar arc Mercury reaches Venus. Hence, this year will bring thoughts (Mercury) of love (Venus) and the decision to enter into a love relationship is in the offing, especially since Venus (together with Moon, Ascendant, Midheaven) is to be found opposite (1). Simultaneously, solar arc Mercury semisquare Sun aspects at (3) the complex of Midheaven, Ascendant, and Venus. Under solar arc Jupiter = Ascendant, we find the search for happiness (Jupiter) with another person (Ascendant).

Not far from this position we see Herta's Mars, which most certainly contributed a great deal to the decision to get married. Solar arc Venus opposite the Moon intensifies the feelings of love.

We see very similar correlations resulting from the directions in Herta's natal chart. Venus semisquare Mars activates the sexual instinct, the longing for a sex partner. Solar arc Ascendant opposition Mars in connection with the Midheaven and Venus intensifies this tendency. Solar arc Sun over Pluto and the Moon of the partner brings about a fervent desire for marriage. We can assume that in this case the woman was the more definite partner in the desire for marriage. In recent years solar arc Pluto has been located opposite the complex of Venus with Ascendant and Midheaven and therefore most likely played a role in solidifying the relationship. It is obvious from all this that Herta, with regard to sex and instinct, was the stronger element, which eventually lead to the decision to marry. However, whatever Pluto has a hand in consolidating usually doesn't last long. This applies also to this case; seven years later the relationship turned completely cold.

Chapter Two

An Introductory Example

We should now take a look at the solar arc directions for Herta and Manfred after seven years. In this period many a crisis occurs, which when overcome is a good thing; but as often as not, if only one of the partners makes a mistake, there is danger of divorce.

Let us first consider Herta's directional picture. Figure 5 presents the two rings of the 90° system. At the very top we see the solar arc Moon's Node aspecting Moon, Venus, Ascendant, and Midheaven. This could be conducive to a more profound love relationship, but it could just as well result in a new love relationship. Solar arc Mars aspecting Mercury indicates conflict and altercations. Solar arc Neptune is in opposition to the Moon's Node.

We should now recall points (4) and (5) in the contact cosmogram in the light of which the undermining of the relationship seems probable. At this juncture, solar arc Venus over Pluto is of special interest. Let us also remember that the relationship came into being under solar arc Pluto = Venus. It is therefore to be expected that Herta will experience a period of strong sexuality, which could result in an extramarital escapade if her relationship with her husband is no longer so intense. In addition, solar arc Moon is approaching Pluto, bringing to mind the position in the

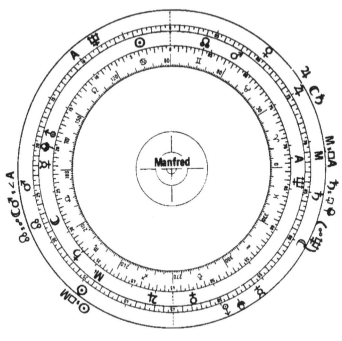

Figure 5

contact cosmogram at (9). Furthermore, solar arc Mercury enters into an aspect to Jupiter, from which we may conclude that certain amenities do not involve the husband because his Saturn is located at this point. Solar arc Sun opposes her own Neptune in the 90o circle and her husband's Mars, pointing to her own disappointment as well as to differences with her husband.

On the right side, solar arc Uranus aspects Mars. According to this configuration, there could be a great upset ahead or even physical intervention through a surgical operation or an accident. However, since in the contact cosmogram the husband's Mars is opposite (6), there is greater likelihood of serious altercations to come.

In Manfred's directional cosmogram we see solar arc Mars aspected with the Ascendant, whereby the points in the contact

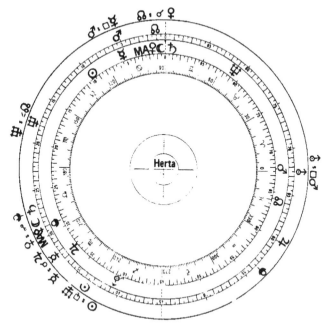

Figure 6

cosmogram around (6) and (8) become involved as well. Conflict (Mars) in the personal environment (Ascendant) becomes likely. Since the solar arc Midheaven comes to a halt at the Ascendant on the other side, personal affairs are also concerned.

The Moon's Node aspecting the Moon should actually be regarded as positive. The Moon is located at the midpoint of Mercury/Saturn and Mars/Neptune, a very unfavorable situation. The solar arc Sun aspecting the Midheaven affects personal affairs, and since Mars is opposite, there is the strong possibility of altercations. Mars and the Midheaven are semisquare in the natal chart. Very critical is the position of solar arc Saturn in the vicinity of Neptune, which already made its appearance in the contact cosmogram as a factor of disappointment.

Before that, however, solar arc Saturn semisquare Pluto becomes due, indicating unusual tension. In the natal chart we find Pluto = Mercury/Uranus, which under certain circumstances can signify nervous irritation. If Saturn turns up at this position, then there is the urge "to find release from tension; the sudden elimination of inhibitions through quick action, the correct grasp of a difficult situation and corresponding self-assertion, separation (bringing oneself into safety)."

Continuing our investigation of this planetary picture, we discover Pluto amidst Venus/Mars = Neptune. On the one hand this means the activation of sexuality, and on the other hand the denial of physical satisfaction. And if solar arc Saturn joins in as well, a separation of the love relationship can be the result. This elaboration should make it obvious that not only are the individual aspects the object of investigation but that the "cosmic state" of each of the factors is also involved in the essential questions.

And what did happen?

According to Herta's story, one evening around 1:00 a.m. she asked a male acquaintance to accompany her to her home because she was afraid of her husband. The acquaintance went along and, in the event of an argument, intended to take the husband to task. At this time the husband was already in bed; however, he was sleeping in the children's room since the couple had for some time stopped sharing the bedroom. The husband heard the two coming, got up, and went into the living room, but no one was there. He then went to his parents' home, and took his father along with him to the police station at about 2:15 a.m. There, he asked for help and for the police to come to his home; but this was refused. In order not to cause a disturbance, father and son waited until the next morning to return to the son's home in the company of two private witnesses.

It was only after a long while that the wife consented to open the door to the bedroom, where she appeared to be alone. The husband looked around the room and suspected that his wife's lover was in the locked wardrobe. He demanded to have the wardrobe opened, or would force it open himself. He then tried to turn over the wardrobe. This turned out to be too much for the man inside, who came out, only to be hit in the face by the husband. Two police officers came in answer to a telephone call. They took Herta's lover with them to the station because he had no identification papers on him. But before he was taken away, he embraced and kissed the wife.

However, severe consequences were in store for the husband as well because the lover was hit more than once, and spent several weeks in the hospital. The husband's fist nearly knocked out one eye, and the man was close to becoming blind. The husband was found guilty of bodily injury and sentenced, and as a result lost his chance to obtain a proposed promotion.

Only on reviewing the preceding events are we able to arrive at the correct interpretation of the Saturn direction in the husband's natal chart. Looking again at the natal Saturn, we find that it is located not only at Moon/Midheaven (emotional inhibitions, pessimism, the undermining of relationships with loved ones, separation, sorrow) but also at Mercury/Jupiter (breakdown in negotiations, saying farewell) = Venus/Pluto (tragic love) = Venus/Uranus (alienation, separation) = Moon's Node/Ascendant (isolation, separation). This entire complex now combines with Neptune = Mercury (improper behavior leads to error and failure) = Sun/Jupiter (undermining of health, material loss) = Venus/Moon's Node (poor prospects ahead for a relationship) = Moon/Mars (undermining of the family).

The contact cosmogram is presented again in Figure 7, with the addition of the daily configurations for the marriage and the scandal, marked in the center. Significant is the triggering of the complex at points 1-3 in the contact cosmogram by the transiting Sun. Transiting Jupiter was located at point (9), and Venus was approaching Manfred's Jupiter. Of importance in connection with

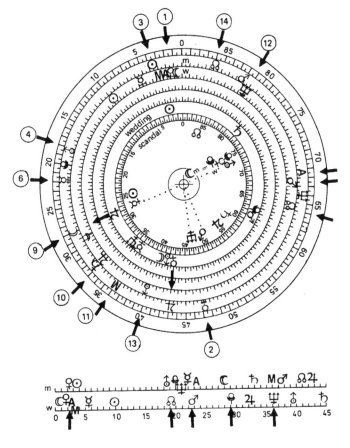

Figure 7

the scandal is the aspect of transiting Uranus with point (9) that triggered the emotional upset and shock already indicated in the contact cosmogram. Transiting Neptune aspects both Venus positions, and transiting Mars acts as trigger at point (3) where the husband's Sun and the wife's Midheavens are located.

We see from this discussion that the important and decisive events in life are indicated by the solar arc directions and that, in

16

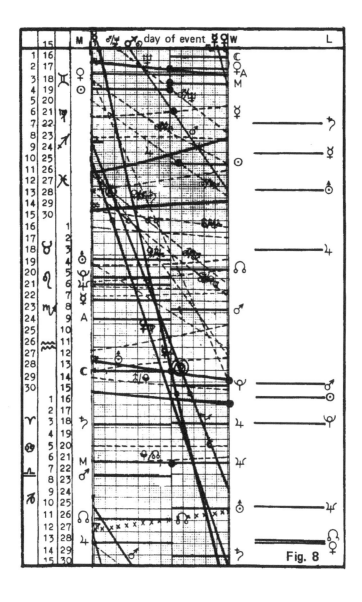

Figure

17

contrast, the transits, measured with the significance of an event, do not always contribute as much as one might suppose. Nonetheless, it is worthwhile reviewing the critical event in the light of the graphic 45° ephemeris (Figure 8).

On the left-hand side of the excerpt from the graphic 45° midpoint ephemeris we find the graduated scale alongside of which the positions of the male cosmogram are entered under "M." The vertical line with the heading "day of the event" marks the day on which the critical incident took place. The positions of the female cosmogram and those of the lover's cosmogram have been entered under "W" and "L."

Neptune's orbit coinciding with the Venus positions of the married couple is immediately evident. Accordingly, this configuration indicates love going astray, disappointment in love, and the undermining of a love relationship. Directly underneath we find the midpoint Mars/Neptune intersecting Manfred's Sun and Herta's Midheaven, signaling the disruption of the personal relationship. Transiting retrograde Jupiter had crossed over Herta's solar position a few days previously, and now the midpoint Mars/Saturn reaches Herta's Sun, corresponding to separation (Mars/Saturn) from males (Sun). At the present time, transiting Saturn has no direct contact with the cosmograms of the couple.

Just below the center we find the decisive configuration. Uranus in transit passes over Manfred's Moon (excitement, upset due to a woman) and approaches Herta's Pluto. Thus the constellation of "emotional (Moon) upset (Pluto)" according to point (9) in the contact cosmogram is again triggered. We see from the "V" in the solar orbit that it is almost a Full Moon, and thus the husband's state of excitement becomes all the more understandable. Venus transited Herta's Pluto shortly before the event. The midpoint Uranus/Pluto coincides exactly with Herta's Pluto. Further below, the midpoint Pluto/Moon's Node transits Manfred's Midheaven. The corresponding statement from *The Combination of Stellar Influences* is interesting in this connection: "The frequent dependence of a person's future upon associations and contacts with others. Associations will often influence one's objectives in life and cause setbacks in one's vocation." The husband suffered a setback of several years, as he was denied his civil service promotion because of the incident. Herta's Neptune is located at the same position, as the wife also suffered from her actions.

The Lover's Cosmogram

We only have the date of birth for the lover and thus will make do with the mid-day positions from the ephemeris. In order to define the purely personal relationship, we would need the Moon,

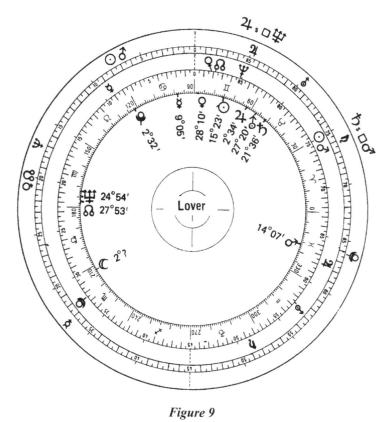

Figure 9

which could aspect the wife's Pluto, Midheaven, and Ascendant, but are of course missing here. The calculation of the directions for the day of the event shows Saturn together with Mars opposition the approaching Sun. This makes the seriousness of the event evident. The fact that this man had to stay in the hospital for many weeks only goes to show how hard the husband must have hit him. Jupiter aspecting Neptune signifies "apparent good fortune" followed by hard reality.

With the woman, the contact cosmogram (Figure 10) shows at point (1) the aspect of Manfred's Venus = Herta's Saturn. This

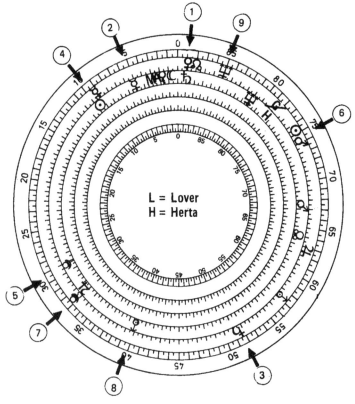

Figure 10

configuration is very frequently involved in cases of illegitimate relationships. At (2) there is a separation indicated by Herta's Mercury with Manfred's Saturn (3); at (4) Manfred's Mercury = Sun is a sign of good understanding; Herta's Pluto at (5) and Sun, and Manfred's Mars at (6) indicate an act of violence, as was actually experienced on the day of the events in question. Manfred's Pluto = Jupiter at (7) shows there was mutual happiness; however, Herta's Uranus (8) and Manfred's Neptune (9) are significators of a state of confusion to come.

Reference should be made to an observation I have often been able to make but which others appear not to mention in their investigations: The midpoints Venus/Mars very frequently coincide with one another in the 90° circle with lovers, and this is also the case here. In addition, with the wife, Neptune is located at the midpoint Venus/Mars, indicating either a love life gone astray or diseases of certain organs. With Manfred we also find Neptune = Venus/Mars, but at another position—points (6) and (7) in the contact cosmogram of the married couple.

Let us now turn to the graphic 45° midpoint ephemeris. At the very right the lover's configurations have been entered (L). These show transiting Mars passing over Saturn shortly after the day of the event. Although transiting Jupiter crosses Mercury, it is simultaneously conjoined with the midpoint Mars/Saturn so that Jupiter at this time can be said to be in very poor cosmic state. At this point we find the aspect to Herta's Sun. Transiting Saturn approaches Uranus. Mars and the Sun provide a connection between the lover's cosmogram and both Manfred and Herta as well—namely a relationship to the questionable point (9) in the contact cosmogram of the couple. The lover's Mars and the wife's Pluto coincide. Just before the event, transiting Venus over the Mars-Pluto aspect indicates the night of love that results in a rude awakening since transiting Uranus approaches Mars (= Herta's Pluto), and transiting Pluto approaches the Sun of the lover. The violence indicated by the transiting bodies is in direct correlation with the direction solar arc Saturn = Mars.

On reviewing the investigation at hand, many more details of which would be worthy of further discussion, we determine the following:

1. The contact cosmogram is an excellent diagramatic method for delving into the relationship of two or more persons to one another.

2. The contact cosmogram is not a static basis of research, but, like the cosmogram itself, it is also subject to changes brought about by the transits and directions.

3. A joint stimulation of events can only occur when the orb of the mutually coinciding positions is kept small. The difference between the mutual points should not exceed one degree. A possible exception to this would be where entire complexes are interrelated, and therefore individual factors will be found to be located at the midpoints of the other cosmogram.

4. Prerequisite to the utilization of the contact cosmogram is the investigation of the individual cosmograms, making it possible not only to examine the relationships among the individual factors, but also to determine their cosmic condition.

5. The primary basis for the stimulation of mutual configurations are the directions that develop.

6. The second basis for the stimulation of mutual constellations are the transits. The transits are best grasped by means of the graphic 45o ephemerides or midpoint ephemerides. These graphic ephemerides make a comprehensive survey of a larger period of time possible and also serve as a kind of living contact cosmogram when the various pages are laid out like playing cards so that the graduated scales and the entries can be looked at simultaneously. In this way we can see which configurations may be jointly stimulated, negatively or positively.

Chapter Three

Famous Couples

For the purposes of illustration I generally use well-known examples because these can easily be checked by anyone who wishes to do so.

Wolfgang von Goethe and Charlotte von Stein

This example was investigated by Dr. H.H. Kritzinger in his *Beitraqen zur Schicksalskunde,* Leipzig 1929. He indicated the positions by merely marking them on the graduated scale of the zodiac and only concentrated on the comparison of certain positions, in particular the trine between the Sun and Mars at 5 Virgo, and the Sun and Mars at 5 Capricorn, and omitting any commentary.

At (1) in the contact cosmogram, the Venus positions of the two very devoted friends coincide, with the addition of Jupiter in Goethe's case. The traditional rule according to which Venus opposition Jupiter is to be regarded as unfavorable is no longer acceptable today. The combination of Sun and Mars at (2) must have led in many instances to upset and conflict, but the Venus-Jupiter relationship was surely stronger as the friendship lasted for very many years. Located opposite at (3), Uranus most certainly was the prompter of much turmoil. At (6) we find the strong combination of Goethe's Sun and Midheaven with Frau von Stein's Mars and

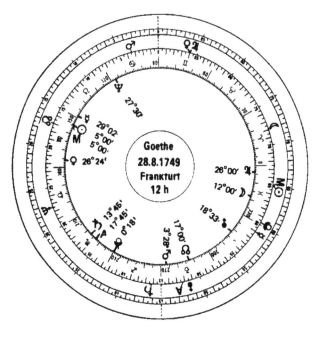

Figure 11

Saturn. This configuration no doubt saved both of them from impulsiveness and aided them in self-control (Saturn).

Frau von Stein's lunar position is not substantiated, but the Moon should be located somewhere in the vicinity of Jupiter. This Jupiter is located precisely in the middle of von Stein's Venus/Mars and Venus with Jupiter and the Sun with Goethe's Midheaven. The strong mutual attraction resulting from this is intruded upon by the midpoint Venus/Saturn (3), and their passion is thus kept within bounds.

The contact cosmogram, of course, must also mirror what takes place in the course of several years. At the time of Goethe's and Frau von Stein's meeting in 1775, Jupiter retreated from 17 to 13 Gemini and thereby formed a relationship to the configuration just

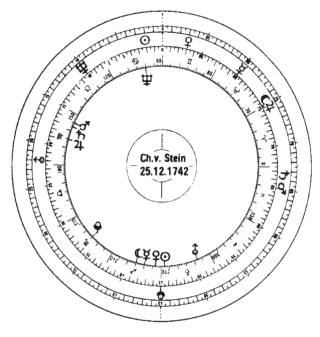

Figure 12

under discussion, i.e., to Jupiter = Venus/Mars = Venus/Saturn (3) and Venus, Jupiter/Sun, Goethe's Midheaven.

The year 1781 is said to have been a turning point in their relationship, of which there has been no explication on the side of the historians to date. From the cosmobiological standpoint, however, any discord in the relationship is comprehensible because transiting Neptune crossed the Sun-Mars combination (2) at that time. Saturn transited Jupiter located at the midpoint (5) several times previously. The differences were overcome, but the relationship was no longer as deep and close as it had been. In 1827, Frau von Stein died. At this time, Pluto transited Goethe's Mars and von Stein's Sun. The discord in 1781 caused by Neptune could be eliminated, but Pluto now represented a *force majeure* that no individual can conquer.

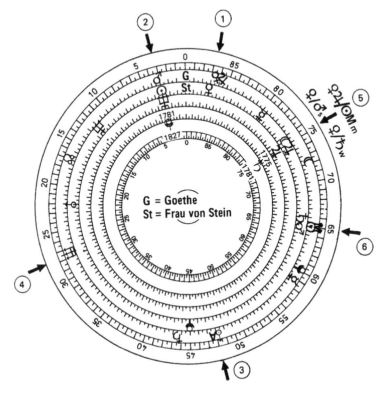

Figure 13

Wolfgang von Goethe and Christiane Vulpius

In the year 1788, Goethe met a young girl, Christiane Vulpius. She could by no means be compared with the highly intellectual and educated Charlotte von Stein; instead, she was the one who took care of his household and saw to his well being. She nursed him devotedly when he was ill and meant more to the great poet and writer, despite her modesty and simplicity, than had first been presumed. A year after they met she gave birth to his son, but since the Weimar society did not consider her to be his equal, it was sixteen years later, in 1806, before Goethe married her.

Figure 14

On considering the contact cosmogram, we immediately notice at (1) the relationship of Goethe's Moon to Vulpius' Sun and Moon's Node. At a distance of a mere two degrees we see Vulpius' Venus, and this is enough in itself to enable us to speak of a strong physical (Sun) and spiritual (Moon-Venus) relationship.

At (2), Moon and Mars are in opposition to one another but without any direct connection with any of the man's factors. But looking more closely, we find that Vulpius' Mars is located in the middle of Goethe's Venus/Mars and Mars/Jupiter, and accordingly, the Moon should also be located at the same midpoints, joined by Saturn/Ascendant and Saturn/Uranus. The initial configurations point to a strong, physical attraction: (Mars = Venus/Mars) and a happy relationship (Vulpius' Moon, Mars = Goe-

27

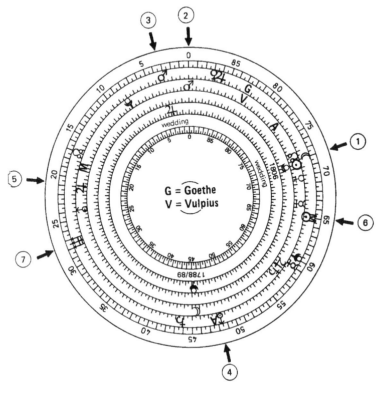

Figure 15

the's Mars/Jupiter). However, other configurations give an indication of pronounced tensions in the relationship (Vulpius' Mars, Moon = Saturn/Ascendant, Saturn/Uranus). It is, however, significant that Pluto was located in this very same constellation in 1788 and 1789 and that, correspondingly, a son came of the passionate relationship.

At (3) and (4), Goethe's Mars and Uranus are in opposition. This axis can be found at the midpoints of Mars/Pluto and Ascendant/Midheaven (assuming these points to be correct), most likely resulting in a great deal of tension. This tension was for the most part alleviated in 1806 by the fact that after many years of living

28

together the decision was made to get married. At this time transiting Jupiter was at position (3). A certain amount of compulsion was most likely also involved. Pluto also played a role in bringing about this late marriage, at the time transiting the two heavenly bodies embodying man and woman, Goethe's Moon and Vulpius' Sun (1). There are indications of the many misunderstandings, insults, and hostility that continually arose through Goethe's Neptune at (7) opposite the positions around (1).

Vulpius' Jupiter (5) with Goethe's Sun and Midheaven (6) is a very strong combination indeed, so that the mutual relationship can be regarded as being happy even if observers thought otherwise. Christiane's death in the year 1816 was a very heavy blow for Goethe.

Emperor Franz Joseph and Elisabeth of Bavaria

The marriage between the young Emperor Franz Joseph I of Austria and Elisabeth of Bavaria is said to have been very unhappy. The main reason for this was that Elisabeth was unable to adjust to the conditions at the Viennese court. The marriage took place in 1854, but the successor to the throne was not born until 1858.

At (1), Franz Joseph's Mars and Elisabeth's Sun form a relationship. This configuration corresponds more to a combat team than to a harmonious marriage. Elisabeth's Sun at Moon/Neptune indicates great sensitivity and probably a low degree of impulsiveness.

At the same time, Franz Joseph's Mars = Mercury/Neptune corresponds to resolute planning and clear-sighted thinking, so that the young emperor was very likely often annoyed by his sensitive wife. His Jupiter and Pluto (2) are opposition his Sun and Elisabeth's Saturn (3), and the female Saturn again represents a strongly inhibitive factor that hinders any true affection. Here we see Moon and Saturn close together in both cosmograms, and at the same time Elisabeth's Venus almost coincides with Franz Jo-

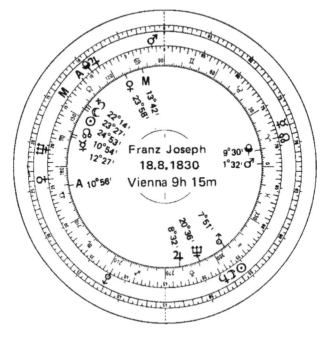

Franz Joseph
18.8.1830
Vienna 9h 15m

Figure 16

seph's Saturn. At the time of Elisabeth's marriage at age seventeen, solar arc Neptune reached to within one degree of a square to
her own Saturn and to her partner's Moon and Sun. These are constellations strongly foreboding of disappointment, which is hardly
a likely foundation for a successful marriage.

A very decisive combination is represented by (4) Franz Joseph's Midheaven with Elisabeth's Pluto and opposition her
Moon. This constellation entered his Venus/Mars and could
arouse enough of an attraction for a successor to the throne to be
born four years later: the unfortunate Crown Prince Rudolf. The
female midpoint Venus/Mars also coincides with Midheaven,
which is square to Jupiter. Rudolf was born when this constellation
by means of a directional arc of 21° was transiting the axis of Franz
Joseph's Jupiter-Pluto (2) opposition Elisabeth's Saturn = Franz

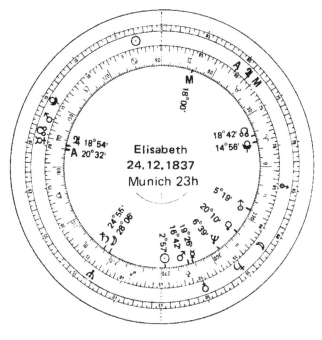

Figure 17

Joseph's Sun (3). However, the mother's inclination for states of depression was inherited by the son, who later committed suicide.

Another disappointment configuration is Franz Joseph's Neptune = Elisabeth's Mercury (6) and with her Uranus (7) in opposition. From the combination of Franz Joseph's Uranus = Elisabeth's Neptune (8) we may conclude that the relationship is unclear, mysterious, confused, and difficult in its definition. This configuration is located approximately at the midpoint of the planetary relationships at (6) and (3).

The death of the Crown Prince on January 30, 1889, was a severe blow for the couple. Elisabeth was age fifty-two at the time. Advancing her Sun by fifty-two degrees, we find it reaches the square to Saturn, which is connected with Franz Joseph's Sun. In

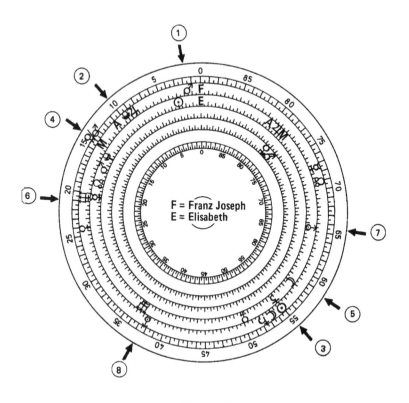

Figure 18

addition, at that time solar arc Saturn reached Mars, which was square to Pluto.

Elisabeth was assassinated September 10, 1898, the Mars-Pluto configuration in the natal chart having been stimulated. This combination often implies the possibility of death through mishap, assassination, or *force majeure*. A marriage of torment was thus also terminated.

Shah Muhammad, Soraya, and Farah Diba

The tragic turn taken by the relationship between Shah Mu-
hammad Riza Pahlavi of Iran and Soraya ("seven-star constellation") Esfandiari Bakhtieri was well exploited by the daily press,
so it will suffice to mention here that there was a very strong love
bond between the two. But the marriage had to be terminated by
divorce, since it brought forth no children.

In the cosmogram, Soraya's Sun (1) and the Shah's Jupiter (2)
oppose one another in the middle of the two Venus positions, thus
indicating happiness in love. At (3) we find the midpoint of her
Sun/Venus corresponding to physical (Sun) love (Venus), opposite his Mercury and Jupiter and her Moon and Moon's Node (4),
from which we may infer spiritual and physical understanding in a

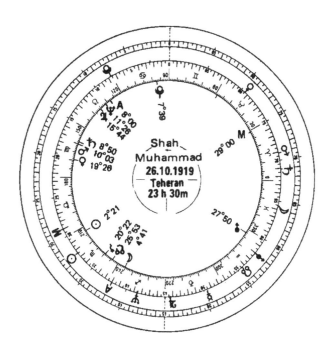

Figure 19

relationship (Moon's Node) with a happy (Jupiter) woman (Moon). However, Soraya's Saturn/Neptune is located at the same midpoint, thus indicating illness in the case of the woman. Love (Venus) thoughts (Mercury) result in a sudden (Uranus) bond (Moon's Node) at points (5) and (6). The opposition of her Pluto (7), her Neptune, and his Moon (8) at the midpoint of her Venus/Saturn points to a relationship of a man to a sick woman. Many persons born around 1932 have the semisquare between Neptune and Pluto in common, but this configuration gains an individual coloring through her Venus/Saturn. Venus/Saturn corresponds to a malfunctioning internal glandular secretion, atrophy, or enlargement. Due to the fact that Neptune and Pluto are also located at this midpoint, there is imminent danger of secretional disorders, i.e., a disturbance in the secretion of certain substances. In the course of time this can lead to a growing coldness in married life, to the real-

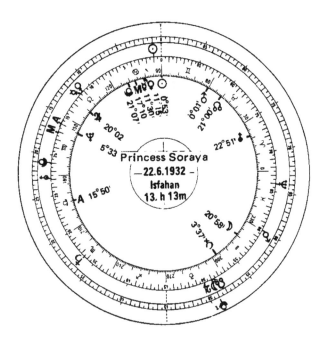

Figure 20

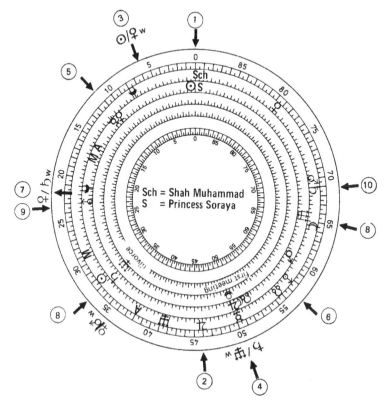

Figure 21

ization that hopes have been disappointed, and to extreme tension or insurmountable difficulties. The danger of a sudden separation is inherent in the opposition of her Uranus (9) and Saturn with Mars (10). His Sun = her Saturn (8) is particularly critical since this may also mean the necessity of a separation.

Two points especially can be considered with regard to the partnership. At the time of the couple's first meeting on October 11, 1950, the marriage taking place a few months later, transiting Pluto stimulated the constellations at (3) and (4), which in Soraya's case were especially significant of a happy relationship.

35

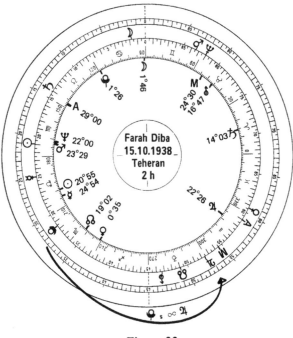

Figure 22

The midpoint of her Sun/Venus (physical love) was triggered simultaneously, but her Saturn/Neptune (illness) became evident after a few months when the expected pregnancy still had not come about. On April 6, 1958, the divorce was proclaimed, when Neptune, destroyer of many hopes and relationships, was located at that position in the contact cosmogram, indicating a later separation, i.e., at his Sun = her Saturn (8) opposite the male Venus.

In May 1959, in Paris, the Shah was introduced to Farah Dibah, one of many Persian students studying architecture there. The engagement was announced November 23, the same year, and the wedding took place in great splendor on December 21, 1959. At the time of the Shah's meeting Soraya, transiting Pluto had aspected Jupiter, and here, too, the direction of Pluto opposition Jupiter was due. But let us first take a look at the contact

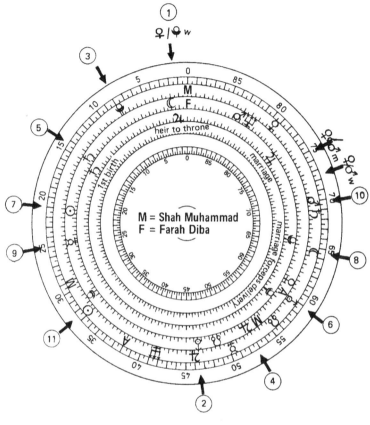

Figure 23

cosmogram itself. Here we make the surprising, but not at all unusual discovery that similar aspects evolve. time and again, even when a change of partners is taking place.

At the location of Soraya's Sun in the contact cosmogram we find Farah Dibah's Moon (1) opposite the Shah's Jupiter. Since Farah Dibah's Moon = her Venus/ Pluto, motherhood is to be expected. The opposition of the Shah's Pluto (3) and her Jupiter (4) point to joint successes. Her Saturn (5) opposition his Uranus = her Venus (6) corresponds to a sudden mutual attraction, but not without crises. These find their cause in part in the fact that an age difference of nineteen years cannot be easily bridged. The relationship to Soraya was endangered by his Moon = her Neptune (8), her Sun (7) and his Moon (8) opposite one another here. Her Mercury (9) opposition his Mars and Saturn (10) may have been the cause of sad thoughts for the young empress since the Shah was under constant threat of assassination and had been in poor health for many years. Instead of his Sun = her Saturn, as in the case of the relationship to Soraya, we have here his Sun (11) = her Pluto, indicating the endeavor to achieve something jointly and also to maintain power in the state.

Looking at the constellations at the time of the wedding, we find transiting Pluto aspecting her Sun = his Moon. This is to say there was a certain element of combustion involved in the marriage, contracted for the particular aim of providing the Shah with a successor to the throne. In addition, transiting Jupiter is located opposition his Sun = her Pluto. The antithesis of this is the same position in the contact cosmogram around Soraya. In Farah Dibah's case, transiting Jupiter = Pluto meant the elevation in station often mentioned in conjunction with Jupiter-Pluto aspects.

At the royal successor's birth, Jupiter aspected Farah Dibah's Moon (1) and her Uranus = the Shah's Jupiter (2). This meant exceptional happiness for the couple since earlier attempts to produce an heir to the throne had failed. The birth itself was difficult, forceps had to be used, and the young mother was put under deep narcosis. This in turn affected the child, which had to be placed in an incubator immediately after delivery. The physician in charge had warned months before that the narrow pelvis might make a Caesarian necessary. However, the Shah rejected this. It is therefore understandable that positions (5) and (6) became critical. They were the locations of transiting Saturn and Pluto in the contact cosmogram. The birth occurred October 31, 1960 at 11:50 a.m. in Teheran. Although it had been feared that Farah Dibah would be unable to give birth to any more children, she had a daughter in 1963.

In conclusion, as in many other cases, the midpoints Venus/Mars are only two degrees apart.

Edward VIII and Wallis Simpson

On January 20, 1936, Edward, the Duke of Windsor, and the uncle of Queen Elizabeth II, became King of England, the successor of his father, Edward VII. Eleven months later he renounced his regentship in order to marry Wallis Simpson, a twice-divorced woman. His abdication caused a furor and was an opportunity for the Irish Free State to proclaim itself a sovereign state outside the commonwealth. Ireland had, along with other dominions of the commonwealth, sanctioned the proposed marriage.

The marriage took place June 3, 1937, and the Duchess of Windsor later published her memoirs under the title *The Heart Has*

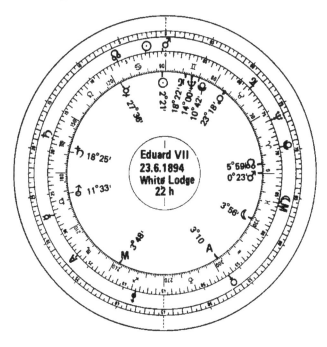

Figure 24

39

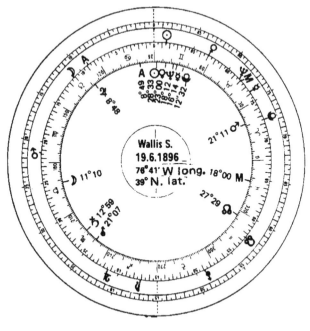

Figure 25

Its Reasons. However, there is a question as to whether it was in truth a love marriage justifying abdication. The cosmic combinations alone cannot give us the full answer to this, but there are several strong correlations to be determined.

The two first met in the winter of 1931, spent a few days of happiness among friends in Biarritz in 1934. They had to postpone their marriage, however, since Wallis Simpson only obtained her divorce in America in 1936.

At the time of their first meeting, Edward was already age thirty-seven and at this time was under the rather intense and invigorating influence of solar arc Venus square Mars. In the case of Wallis Simpson, who was thirty-five, solar arc Jupiter was square to Pluto. Since this is a configuration frequently involved in per-

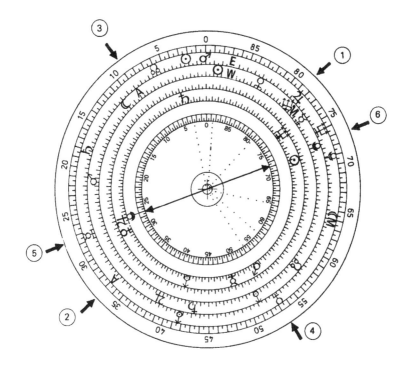

Figure 26
E = Edward VIII; W = Wallis Simpson

sons being elevated in station, we may assume that at the beginning, love was not the only ponderable factor. The possibility of a higher social position was undoubtedly part of the attraction.

At (1) Edward's Jupiter aspects Wallis' Midheaven and Neptune. In Edward's cosmogram we find Jupiter at the midpoints Sun/Moon = Sun/MC = Moon/Mars = Mars/Midheaven, so that we may construe from this combination the possibility of a happy marriage, a positive attitude towards life along with clear-cut aims, honesty and frankness (contributing to the decision to abdicate) and the urge to act according to one's own dictates. Combined with this is not only Wallis' Midheaven but also the midpoint Venus/Pluto, indicating a tendency for a personal and independent standpoint in love problems. We may read Neptune to state that she had no objections to being seduced by this partner (Neptune = Venus/Pluto).

Opposite, along the same axis, his Ascendant (2) and her Ascendant (3) are opposite his Venus (4), which is yet another significator of a very strong love tie. At (5) his Mercury is opposition her Pluto, resulting in attitudes and thinking being reciprocated and also a good spiritual understanding. In addition, Mercury is located at Sun/Venus and Moon/Jupiter as well as at the female midpoint Sun/Moon's Node, greatly intensifying the mutual attraction.

After all the obstacles had been cleared away, and the marriage could take place, the wedding day was under the aegis of Jupiter and Pluto—great happiness—and Sun and Venus were also located close by. The couple always stood together even though life was not easy for them by.

King Baudouin and Queen Fabiola

For many years, the Belgians waited in vain for their king, who often suffered from depression, to marry. He finally succeeded in finding a wife: Fabiola de Mora y Aragon. For two years after their meeting in 1958 he was able to keep his secret, so the announcement of his engagement on September 16, 1960 caused a genuine sensation.

Several solar arc directions fell due for him at this time: solar arc Venus sesquisquare Jupiter, sesquisquare Uranus, and solar arc Venus = Jupiter/Uranus, solar arc Jupiter square Midheav- en, solar arc Uranus opposition Midheaven, solar arc Sun square Jupiter opposition Uranus. At the end of December 1957, I indicated that the Belgian king should take advantage of the good Jupiter transits (transiting Jupiter conjunction Venus) in order to find his life's companion. Is had to wait two years before it was confirmed that King Baudouin had indeed made his choice.

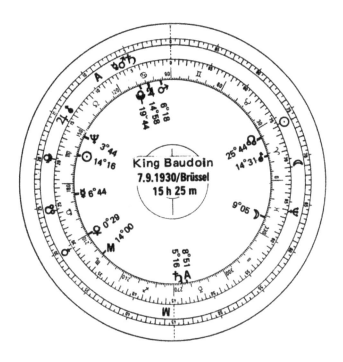

Figure 27

In these years, solar arc Jupiter semisquare Pluto (elevation of station!), solar arc Venus conjunction Pluto, and solar arc Saturn opposition Pluto were due for Fabiola.

On considering the contact cosmogram we immediately notice the critical aspect (1) of his Mercury, Mars and Saturn = her Uranus. There is promise of better prospects through his Jupiter = her Pluto (2). Yet we find a critical configuration in the form of his Pluto = her Mars (3) opposition his Neptune (4), and latent in this combination are hidden causes, unusual problems, illness, love, and emotional suffering. A truly favorable combination is formed by his Venus = her Jupiter (5) and opposition his Sun = her Venus (6), whereby only Saturn next to the female Venus can be regarded as unfavorable.

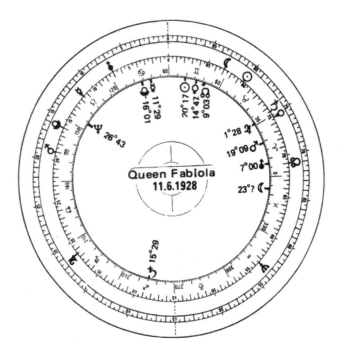

Figure 28

The favorable constellation (5) was triggered by transiting Jupiter and stationary Venus at the time of the first meeting in 1958, and the favorable combination of his Sun = her Venus (6) was involved as well. The same combination was triggered at the time of the engagement on September 16, 1960. At the time of the wedding, transiting Jupiter crossed her Mercury at the midpoints of her Sun/Jupiter and his Mars/Jupiter, which is often a contributory factor at the time of marriage.

Unfortunately, the critical constellations also began to come to the fore in the form of a number of miscarriages, destroying any hopes of an heir to the throne being born. Is have at hand the dates for three miscarriages where the same constellations were repeatedly in action. The strong combination of the complexes (5) and

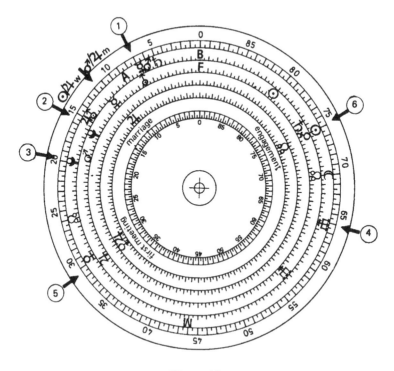

Figure 29
B = Baudouin; F = Fabiola

(6) is triggered at each miscarriage. Even though Sun, Venus and Jupiter point to a happy relationship and a truly deep spiritual bond, Saturn still remains very unpleasant in its influence at this particular position. The contact constellation at (1) was stimulated June 26, 1961, and November 6, 1966, with Baudouin's Saturn being the villain. The great effectiveness of the constellations in July 1966 made the wish for children a vain one.

This case exemplifies especially well the necessity of not only considering the contact cosmogram for itself but also for including in one's investigation the potential effects of the aspects of the years to come.

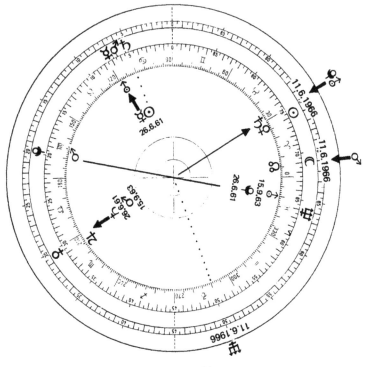

Figure 30

Peter Townsend and Princess Margaret Rose

After his discharge from the military, former British Air Force Group Captain Peter Townsend was installed at the Court in London as Royal Equerry. He served from 1944 to 1952, and one of his duties was to escort Princess Elizabeth (later, Queen Elizabeth II) and Princess Margaret Rose. He was in the company of Princess Margaret at the coronation of the Dutch Queen Juliane and was also Princess Margaret's escort on her father's trip to South Africa.

In 1952 and 1953, Townsend was the Queen Mother's equerry at Clarence House, where Princess Margaret also resided. As the

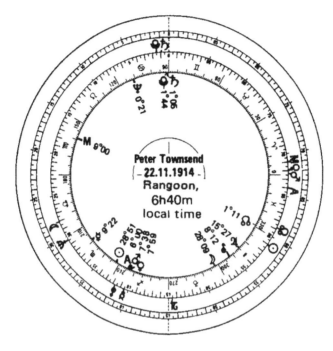

Figure 31

first rumors of a love affair between the princess and Townsend became public in July 1953, Townsend was appointed air attache to the British Embassy in Brussels. Townsend's possible marriage with the princess was out of the question since his 1942 marriage was divorced in 1952, and the Church of England, which is presided over by the Queen, does not recognize any marriage to a divorced person. On October 31, 1955, the Princess made the official announcement that she did not intend to marry Peter Townsend.

The contact cosmogram shows a severe emotional depression related to Townsend's Saturn and Pluto (1) = Midheaven. The actual love contact is comprised of the princess' Venus and Jupiter (2) opposition the solar positions of both partners (3). Because her Mars reached this contact point at age seventeen (1947), we may

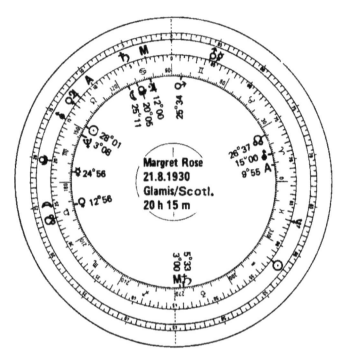

Margret Rose
21.8.1930
Glamis/Scotl.
20 h 15 m

Figure 32

assume that although a strong attraction was already developing, it would be kept secret until 1953. We should not overlook the fact that Venus and Jupiter ware located at her Saturn/Pluto and that this constellation is indicative of self-discipline, renunciation, and alienation. Townsend's Moon (4) coincides with her Moon's Node, which tends to support a relationship. The only significator of disappointment is his Neptune, which is in the vicinity.

The two people have an age difference of sixteen years, which usually leads to difficulties. For this reason, Townsend supported the princess in her decision. The daily configurations during this period are very unusual indeed. Transiting Neptune and Uranus pass over her Moon and Moon's Node, and his Moon and Neptune (4), indicating disappointment and renunciation. However, tran-

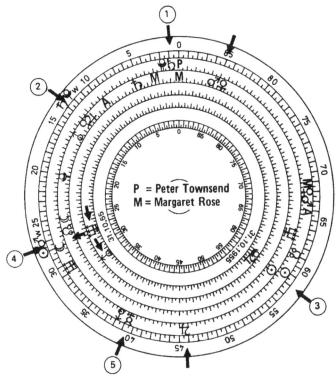

Figure 33

siting Jupiter and Pluto are aspected with the Sun and Venus of both. This combination would actually be counted as positive if we did not have at the same time Venus and Jupiter = Saturn/Pluto, pointing to renunciation, but possibly also meaning success. It seems, however, that the spiritual bond between the two continued to exist for some time afterward. Townsend took his discharge from the Royal Air Force in October 1956, went on a trip around the world, and was married in December 1959, by which time Margaret Rose had also found a new partner.

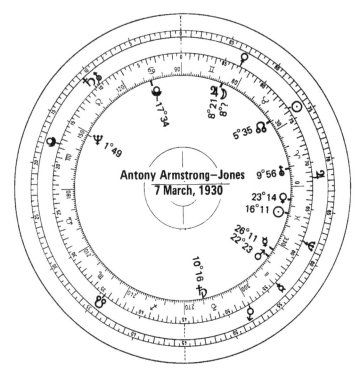

Figure 34

Anthony Armstrong-Jones and Princess Margaret

Anthony Armstrong-Jones was a professional photographer whose life had been filled with bad luck and who had failed several exams, but whose photographic work was a great success. In 1959, he made the official photographic portrait of Princess Margaret on the occasion of her twenty-ninth birthday. At this time, progressed Mars reached the square to Venus in the princess's cosmogram, so she was filled with a great longing for love. With Tony, as he was usually called, solar arc Mars conjunction Venus was due at this time, and a new friendship was welcome. The princess is said to have often visited him secretly disguised in her maid's clothes. But the more incautious she became the more unlikely it became for

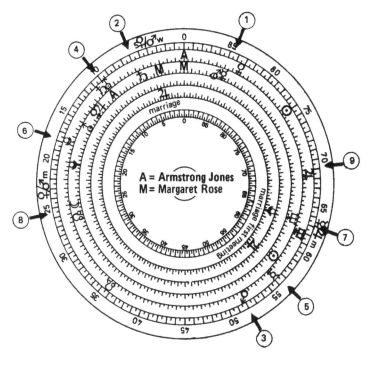

Figure 35

her visits to remain unknown. The engagement was announced February 26, 1960, and the wedding took place May 6, 1960.

The passionate relationship lies in his Venus = her Mars (1) and had already been indicated at the time of their meeting by various directions. Her Saturn (2) and his Mars (3) formed a critical aspect to one another, which was all the more so because her Venus/Mars almost coincided with this axis. His Saturn and Uranus aspecting her Ascendant gave indications of altercations and conflicts, which, if reports were true, had already been borne out. Opposite, his Mercury and her Sun (5) conjoin at her Moon/Mars midpoint. This is the same position at which Townsend's Sun had been located. His Pluto (6) opposition both Neptune positions could have led to disappointment after the stimulation of the passion configuration of her Venus/Pluto. Likewise, his Mercury/Jupiter = Pluto = Neptune at this position was at first positive and then negative in value. Her Moon (8) and his Jupiter (9) were indicative of both partners' happiness, especially at the beginning, when solar arc Mars entered the conjunction to her Moon.

At the time of their beginning friendship, the favorable aspect of his Mercury = her Sun at (5) was triggered by transiting Jupiter. Although transiting Pluto at the time of the marriage was located on the critical axis of his Pluto-her Neptune (7), it was also at the midpoint of his Mercury/Jupiter and her Venus/Pluto. The husband's main aggravation seems to have stemmed from his difficult adjustment to court ceremony and etiquette, which greatly contrasted with the more carefree life he spent as a photographer in artistic circles. by the mid 1970s, the couple was said to have almost completely gone their separate ways, even though a smiling facade was still maintained on official and public occasions, covering up inward suffering. The contact cosmogram can in no way be considered a propitious one, for a relationship based purely on passion, as is probably the case here, does not last long.

The unusual differences in milieu certainly also contributed to the difficulties. The husband, given the title of Earl of Snowdon under solar arc Sun = Pluto, variously tried his hand at different enterprises, but with little success. The couple was divorced in 1978.

Don Juan Carlos and Gabriella of Savoy

Don Juan Carlos, son of Don Juan of Spain, Pretender to the Throne, intended in 1955 to marry Gabriella of Savoy, the daughter of the former king of Italy, Umberto II. The Shah of Persia had also wanted to ask for her hand in marriage, but her father announced in October 1960 that a marriage between Gabriella and Don Juan Carlos was likely. Don Juan's father expressed the wish, however, that the marriage be postponed until he had finished his education.

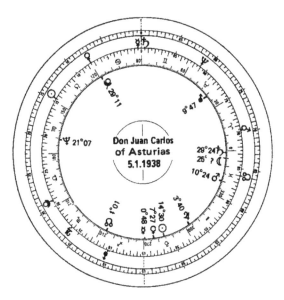

Figure 36

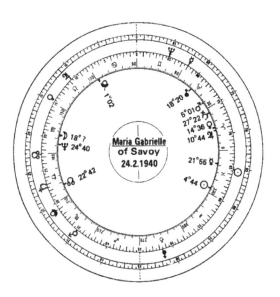

Figure 37

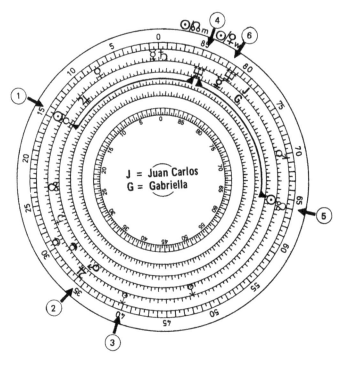

Figure 38

Looking at the contact cosmogram, we find that his Sun = her Venus provides a foundation for a true love relationship. His Jupiter = her Mars points to the bonds of matrimony (2). His Uranus and her Neptune (3/4) give hints of a possible disappointment, especially since they are located at the midpoints of her Sun/Venus and his Sun/Moon's Node (3). His Moon's Node = her Sun (5) relates to an association, but misunderstandings and disappointment could arise through his Neptune = her Mercury (6).

Her Neptune is located between the two configurations of Sun = Venus (1) and Sun = Moon's Node (5). At age twenty, her solar arc Sun reached Neptune and solar arc Neptune reached Venus. Hence Neptune directions have struck the best constellations in the contact cosmogram and thus undermined the relationship.

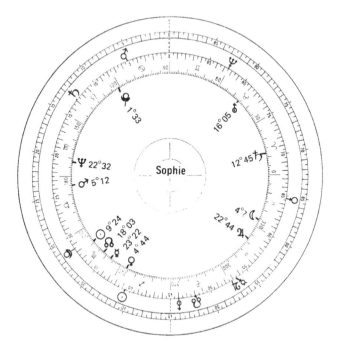

Figure 39

Don Juan Carlos and Sophie of Greece

This contact cosmogram does not appear at first glance to be particularly favorable. It is, however, possible that completely different aims and intentions were involved here. His Mercury (1) = her Uranus (2) can be considered as positive, despite his Saturn since this axis falls between the two favorable constellations (4) and (7). His Venus (3) opposition her Jupiter and Mercury (4) at her Sun/Venus is favorable for a love relationship, which because of his Mars/Jupiter could also lead to marriage. His Venus (3) is little more than two degrees away from her Mars, which, at Venus/Pluto, indicates a strong physical attraction. In contrast, his Sun = her Saturn (5) must be regarded as unfavorable. His Jupiter and her Pluto (6) point to joint successes. Due to his Uranus = her

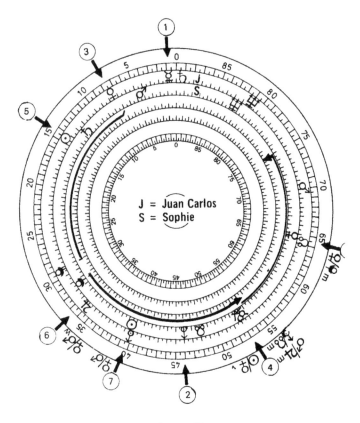

Figure 40

Sun, the couple experienced some upsets. However, the midpoints Venus/Mars located at points (6) and (7) activated a stronger attraction. His Moon's Node = her Venus (8) at his Venus/Pluto is significant of a strong love relationship. Examining the interactions of the directions we find these contributed a great deal toward bringing about the marriage.

Solar arc Venus conjunct with his Pluto indicates a peak of passion. Solar arc Pluto reached the complex of her Jupiter, Mercury and his Venus, meaning one's personal success, i.e., marriage. Solar arc Jupiter and solar arc Mercury made a station opposite her

Pluto, indicating the achievement of an aim in life. A social better-ment, which is usually the case with Jupiter-Pluto aspects had not as yet come into effect. His ascension to the throne came in 1975.

Gerhard Freund and Marianne Koch

Before it occurred, it was widely known the marriage of the ac-tress (and later, physician) Marianne Koch and Gerhard Freund, a physician, was breaking up. The reasons for this break-up are ob-vious. Her work as a film actress made frequent travel necessary, and she had many male co-stars. Her husband apparently did not like being alone, so he began a relationship with Petra Schurmann, a former beauty queen. Gerhard and Marianne had two children. The couple was married in 1953, and divorced in 1973.

Figure 41

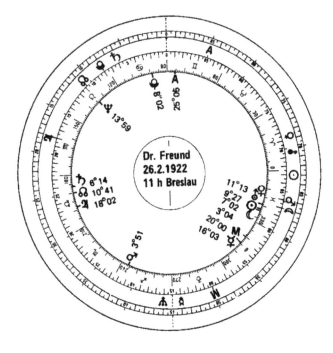

Figure 42

Marianne got her start as an actress in the spring of 1950 and was hired for many motion pictures. Progressed Mars conjunction the Midheaven and solar arc Uranus square Jupiter were probably instrumental in her rapid advancement.

Moon = Venus/Jupiter and Venus = Sun/Moon in her cosmogram are indicative of a happy marriage. Although Neptune = Mercury/Venus provides great powers of imagination and acting talent, it also does not preclude possible disappointment in love.

In Dr. Freund's cosmogram, love life is fostered by Sun = Venus/Mars = Moon/Venus. However, the presence of Venus = Uranus can also mean the danger of amatory adventures and infidelity. Jupiter = Moon/Mars provides the possibility of his being happy

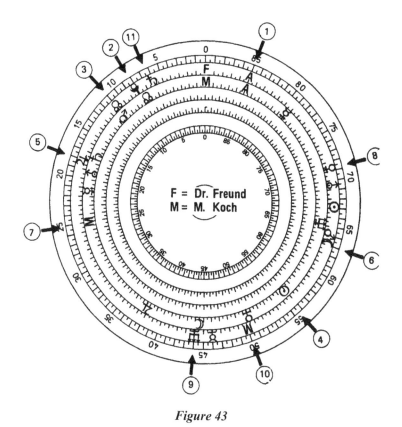

Figure 43

with one woman alone. Neptune = Mercury = Venus/Jupiter indicates the possibility of disappointments ahead.

The contact cosmogram contains many contrasting aspects. The partners have a joint Ascendant in the 90° circle, and actually, the two Ascendants are complements located opposite one another in Gemini and Sagittarius. In the light of (2) his Pluto = her Moon's Node and (3) his Mars opposition her Sun, the union of these two seems to have been predestined. In cases like these, we speak of a karmic union. At (5), the favorable aspect of his Jupiter = Moon/Mars coincides with her Saturn, an early indication of a possible separation.

Her Midheaven and his Venus oppose one another at (7) and (8) and are significators of deep affection and love—at least at the beginning.

At (9), his Neptune = her Moon indicates disappointment and an undermining (Neptune) of the relationship. His Midheaven = her Venus at (10) corresponds to the contact at (7/8). His Saturn = her Moon's Node at (11) relates to the danger of a separation.

The next object of consideration is always to determine how mutual contact points are activated by directions and transiting bodies.

Looking at Marianne Koch's natal chart, we find the following directions forming for the year 1973:

- Solar arc Mars = Venus: passionate love
- Solar arc Midheaven = Neptune: personal disappointment
- Solar arc Moon = Ascendant: acquaintanceship, emotional and spiritual bond
- Solar arc Venus = Moon: the feeling of love

Gerhard Freund's shows:

- Progressed Venus = Neptune: disappointment in love
- Solar arc Neptune = Midheaven: personal disappointment
- Solar arc Mercury = Saturn: thoughts of separation
- Solar arc Ascendant = Moon: ties with others

Looking at the contact cosmogram, we note how the divorce is reflected cosmically: At (9) we find the crux of this mutual disappointment. Solar arc Venus = Moon are due in Marianne's cosmogram where his Neptune was located. Progressed Venus = Neptune falls due where her Moon is located. In addition, this same point was touched by his solar arc Neptune.

The annual diagrams provide further information. A contact cosmogram can again be had by placing the annual diagrams

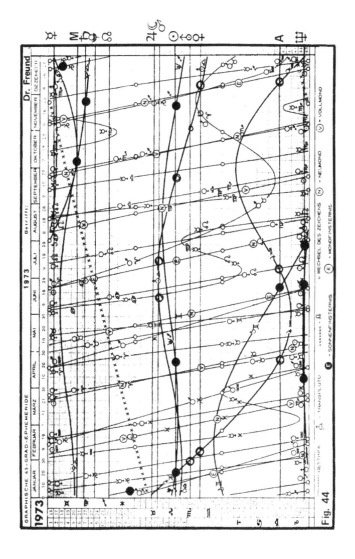

Figure 44

61

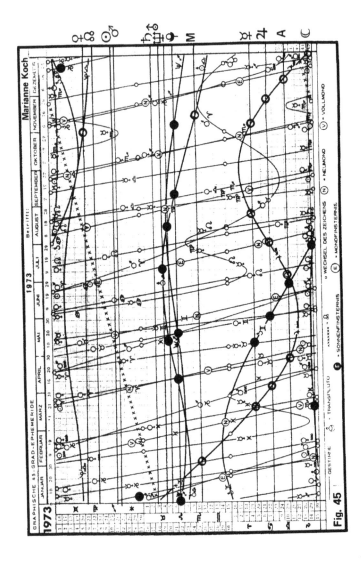

Figure 45

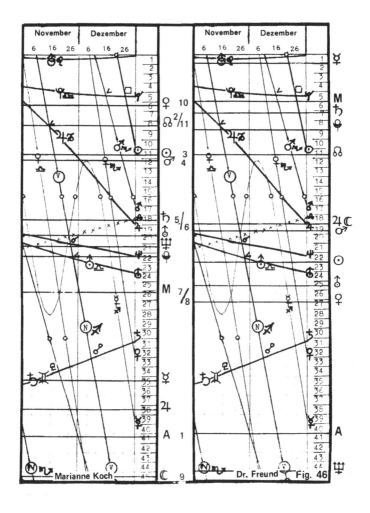

Figure 46

63

alongside of each other, showing up the possibilities of stimulation and resolution. Our illustration presents a section from the 1972 graphic 45° ephemeris. The same numbers as in the contact cosmogram have been entered in the middle. We now only need to make a mental picture of the preceding portion of the graphic representation in order to survey the entire development. We then see how the planets Uranus and Neptune had recently transited the complexes (5/6) in succession. At the very top, Pluto at (10) approached her Venus, indicating a new and strong love relationship, whereas Pluto aspecting his Mercury could mean a significant change in life, one which would not come easily since Saturn is in the vicinity. Financial problems would most likely play an important role in this connection.

Looking at the annual diagrams for 1973, we find that Transpluto in the lower part of the diagram seems to have played a not insignificant role in the divorce; it transits the her Neptune and his Moon, i.e., the disappointment constellations.

In the center, Uranus and Neptune still revolve about the complex (6/6), and greater disadvantages appear at first to be present in her diagram, whereas more are in store in his diagram. At any rate, the gist of the matter is that the critical contact points existing at (5/6) from the very beginning could not be overcome as the slow-moving bodies Uranus and Neptune transited them. Neither of the partners seemed to have done much to solve their differences. Rather, each sought new ties.

Chapter Four

Problem Marriages

For some, marriage can mean torment and even a threat to life when the husband or the wife is sick, perhaps even without his or her knowledge. It is often neglected that some alleged character fault, peculiar behavior, or reaction are as often as not the result of some nervous or organic disorder or can be traced to some psychic disturbance. In such cases, a cosmobiological examination can often clear the way for betterment or remedy.

Sadist and Wife

For the sake of discretion, the exact dates for the following case cannot be given here. However, the essential constellations are so unmistakable that they in themselves give a clear-cut picture of the situation. What first strikes us in the male cosmogram in the 90o circle is the Mercury and Uranus aspect. Even without using any aids we can easily recognize the positioning of Mercury and Uranus at the midpoints Venus/Saturn and Mars/Neptune. This indicates great tensions in the love life, most specifically through narrow-mindedness and selfishness; nervous disorders, possibly due to the indulgence in drugs and alcohol; and through some other pathological state as well. In the 90° circle, Sun and Saturn are in opposition at the midpoints Mars/Uranus and Mercury/Mars. We

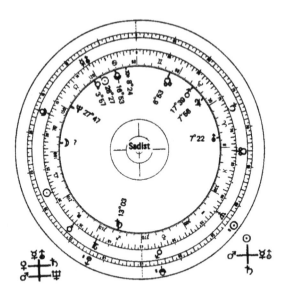

Figure 47

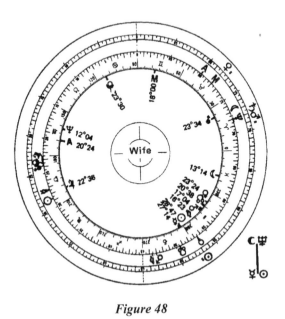

Figure 48

may derive from this an inclination toward violence and ulterior motives. We might interpret Venus at Sun/Jupiter to correspond to a well-balanced and harmonious attitude toward love; however, Venus at Mercury/Neptune indicates an attraction of short duration, and Venus at Uranus/Neptune corresponds to a peculiar or perverted form of love. Mars at Venus/Moon's Node indicates great passion, but we may conclude lack of responsibility from Mars at Jupiter/Neptune.

In this man's chart at the time of the marriage, Mercury was conjunct Uranus over Jupiter, which is located at Sun/Mars. This corresponds to a correct grasp of that situation and to a quick marriage. In the course of the following year, solar arc Pluto was conjunct Mars and therefore indicated unusual effort and achievement or else acts of violence. Solar arc Sun was conjunct Neptune, an indication of disease.

Now looking at the wife's cosmogram, we find the aspect of Moon to Neptune opposition Sun and Mercury to be negative. This bodes hypersensitivity, weakness, disappointment, and emotional suffering. The complex Jupiter-Pluto-Uranus may be regarded as positive, yet it has no individual value because it lacks any connection with other factors in the natal chart. The conjunction of Mars and Saturn is critical.

In the contact cosmogram we find his Mercury and Uranus (1) opposition her Venus (7) meaning a sudden but probably only temporary attraction. The solar positions of both partners coincide (2), but unfortunately they are also in opposition to his Saturn and her Moon and Neptune (3). Hence the most unfavorable configurations of both cosmograms coincide with one another. His Venus (4) opposition her Midheaven (5) is indicative of an individual kind (Midheaven) of love (Venus). His Mars = her Mars and Saturn (6) can be considered to be an extremely critical configuration.

And it is just these very severe configurations which were triggered in the first year of marriage. Solar arc Sun = her Venus and

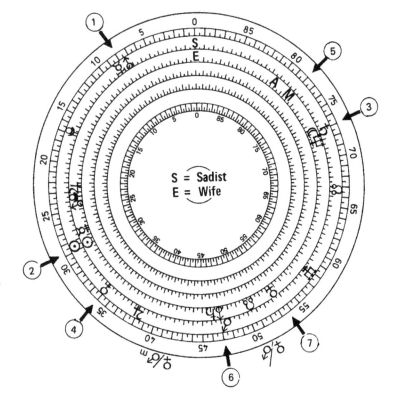

Figure 49

solar arc Venus = her Midheaven signify the love relationship and
the subsequent marriage. However, solar arc Mars and Saturn in
her cosmogram conjoins with the mutually critical constellation at
(2) and (3), and the husband's solar arc Pluto joins the constellation of his Mars = her Mars and Saturn (6). We might also note
here that in the cosmogram of the sadist, progressed Venus approached Saturn, indicating a quick cooling down of the love relationship, and also the mutual constellation at (2) and (3).

When the dates on this marriage were submitted to me, Is care-
fully investigated them and on the basis of this Is recommended a

quick divorce, which was in fact promptly granted. The torments the wife suffered from her sadistic husband are almost indescribable. (By sadism Is mean the urge to obtain sexual gratification by humiliating, inflicting pain upon, and even killing another person.) The husband tortured his wife, he threatened to "fix" her for life, he took away all the money she had, even what she earned herself. He had also become a heavy drinker and was especially brutal when he had imbibed too much alcohol. She was so much in fear of her husband that she wouldn't dare say even a few words to her mother. It was her mother who finally took the necessary steps to free her daughter from her marital torture.

How could such a marriage as this come about? It seems the husband, outwardly at least, made a very good impression (Venus = Sun/Jupiter). He was a so-called Prince Charming, one you could only see through as time went by. In this case the contact cosmogram would certainly have opened their eyes in time, and daughter and parents would have been able to put a stop to the marriage.

Neurotic Husband

These questions were asked in regards to the charts: Would a child be born during a certain time? Would the husband's promotion be a cause for joy? Did the husband kill his wife while temporarily insane? The fact that it is possible to anticipate an impending crisis proves that preventive measures would have been practicable.

Looking at each cosmogram for itself, we see that Mars and Saturn are across from one another in the 90° circle in both charts; the aspect is the sesquiquadrate. The husband has another sesquiquadrate between Mercury and Neptune at the midpoints Moon/Pluto, Pluto/Midheaven, and Venus/Jupiter, indicating both an enervating relationship and a mental disorder, assuming other indications in this direction are present as well. Finally, Venus and Pluto are in opposition, joined by the Ascendant, so that we have

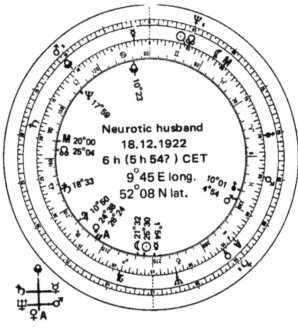

Figure 50

the following planetary picture: Pluto-Venus, Ascendant = Mercury/Saturn = Mars/Neptune.

This represents fanatic love, separation in love, unusual love problems, false attitudes in love, and, according to *The Combination of Stellar Influences*, "the tendency to cause damage to others brutally or to suffer likewise (dissolution, death)."

This configuration nearly coincides with Mars-Saturn in the woman's natal chart. Taking an orb of 2°, yet another sesquiquadrate can be found between Saturn and Venus, or Saturn at the midpoint Venus/Mars can be determined. In either case, suffering in love, marital crises, and perhaps even separation are indicated. Moon aspecting Neptune in a woman's natal chart has proved to be unfavorable in its influence on a marriage. Here we find Moon

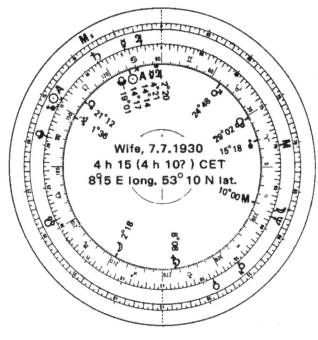

Figure 51

and Neptune at Mars/Midheaven = Venus/Midheaven and opposition Sun = Uranus = Saturn/Pluto. The implications of this are emotional and mental upset, low self-assertive ability, dissatisfaction, unhappiness, self-torture, and suf- fering a blow of fate.

We now set up the contact cosmogram to facilitate our investigation of the relationship. His Mercury and her Jupiter coincide at (1), which is basically an indication of a good mutual relationship, and this was most likely the case in the beginning at least. According to the reports of these living in the house, the married couple in question lived in general harmony. Only Neptune opposite (2) points to disappointment.

His Pluto (3) opposition his Venus m and her Mars shows unusually strong passion in the husband which can develop into bru-

71

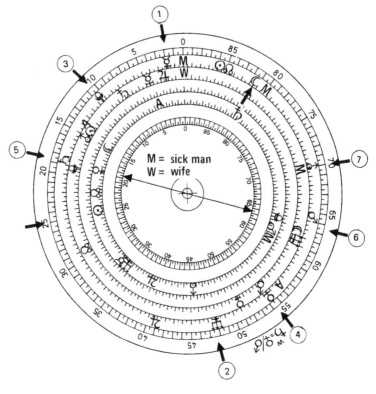

Figure 52

tality (his Pluto = her Mars). As has been shown above, the approximate aspect of his Pluto = his Venus is at Mars/Neptune.

His Saturn = her Pluto (5) combined with his Mars (6) can trigger brutality and the will to destroy according to the corresponding directions or transits. His Uranus = her Midheaven (7) may be interpreted to mean continual upset in the woman's life.

What happened? On October 18, 1958, the couple had put the children to bed and was about to pay relatives a visit. Tenants in the house heard a loud exchange of words around 8.40 p.m., The radio was playing loudly. Suddenly, out of the living room came the words: "Karl, what are you doing? " Because there was no an-swer to the door-bell, the front door to the apartment was opened by force. The wife was found with an almost three-inch cut across the carotid artery. Meanwhile the husband had made a wild escape out the window and run away. The five-year-old son heard his mother's calls for help but came too late, and she died before the physician could do anything to help her. The husband threw him-self in front of a train.

Could these terrible events have been foreseen? The answer must be yes. Look at Figure 53, which presents a section from the graphic midpoint ephemerides for the month of October 1958. The thick position lines are those of the husband, and the dotted lines are the wife's position lines. As we can see at the very top, transit-ing Uranus approached his Mercury = her Jupiter. This configura-tion was not yet due, but it nevertheless has to be included in our considerations since transits are generally triggered beforehand.

This constellation tells us: "suddenly misguided imagination, convulsive disturbances in connection with the nervous system" (*The Combination of Stellar Influences*). At this position we also find the midpoint Mars/Neptune transiting his Neptune and her Jupiter.

A bit farther down we find the midpoint Mars/Uranus aspecting her Mars and Saturn and his Venus and Pluto (3/4). This implies a high degree of passion and excitation with severe consequences.

Transiting Mars, which at the time was slow-moving and in perigee, was not very far away from transiting Pluto. This results in transiting Mars = her Moon and transiting Pluto = his Saturn = her Pluto (5/6). The possibility of a violent act as anticipated be-comes a fact.

Transiting Sun = his Uranus = her Midheaven corresponds to the sudden and drastic event. In the lower part of the graphic repre-sentation we note transiting Neptune approaching her Midheaven and transiting Saturn approaching his Moon. This is an additional

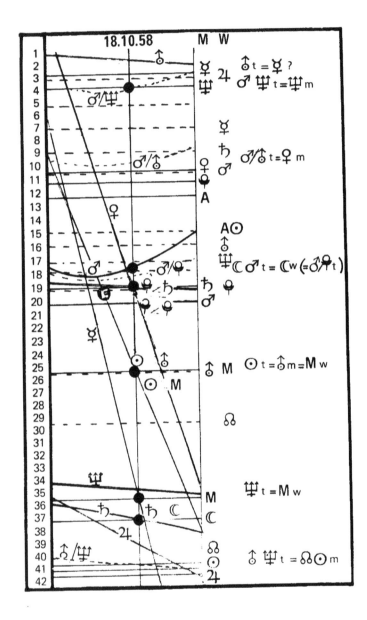

Figure 53

indication of critical times ahead during which the wife would lack energy and the power of resistance (Neptune = Midheaven), and the husband would possibly face separation (Saturn) from the wife (Moon). Since his Moon is located at Mars/Pluto in the natal chart, this correlates to the injury (Mars/Pluto) of a woman (Moon), while transiting Saturn at this position may also be connected with suicide.

In the inner circle of the contact cosmogram the transiting positions are given as well so that they may be compared with Figure 53. One has to admit that it was just those critical contact points which appeared on comparison of the two charts which were triggered in the tragic affair.

This question now arises: Can marital crises be anticipated?

Usually the married couple's annual diagrams are compared in order to determine when positive or negative events involving both partners are likely to occur. A survey covering several years is only possible by means of the life diagram, which involves the graphic representation of the progressed aspects according to the correspondence of one day of life = one year of life. Accordingly, the twentieth day of life after the day of birth corresponds to the twentieth year of life, the thirty-sixth day after birth the thirty-sixth year of life, and so on.

In the consideration of the individual natal charts, one's attention should particularly be directed to the positions lying close together that can be triggered by further progression, be it forward or backward. In the husband's natal chart, Mercury and Neptune are sesquiquadrate. Since Neptune is retrograde, progressed Neptune can reach Mercury.

The period covering the thirtieth to fortieth year of life, i.e., from 1952 to 1962, is given in Figure 54 on the basis of the progressed movement of the heavenly bodies. Here we note how progressed Neptune gradually approached Mercury. In addition, progressed Jupiter and progressed Mars were also approaching this

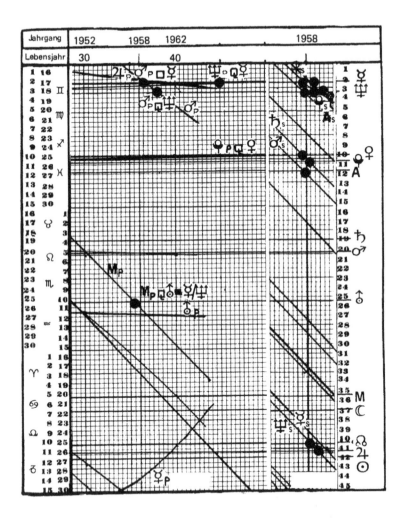

Figures 54 (left) and 54A (right)
Section from husband's life diagram;
progressions; solar arc directions

combination of Mercury-Neptune in the natal chart. These config-urations become due around the year 1958. Accordingly, there was the possibility of "disturbances which originate in the subcon-scious, self-deception, lack of clarity, inner confusion" (*The Combination of Stellar Influences*) being triggered.

Approximately in the center of the picture we see the pro-gressed Midheaven over Uranus = Mercury/Neptune. Hence it is possible that the "misguided imagination" or "convulsive distur-bances in connection with the nervous system" contained in the natal chart may be triggered by progressed Midheaven (*The Combination of Stellar Influences*).

The solar arc directions are similarly presented in Figure 54. Solar arc Venus, solar arc Pluto, and the solar arc Ascendant were transiting the same position as Mercury and Neptune in the natal chart, making clear the connection between nervous disorders and love-life and also indicating the probability of unusual actions.

Lower down, solar arc Saturn transits Venus and Pluto, and so-lar arc Mars transits the Ascendant, pointing to the danger of a sep-aration in love (Saturn = Venus) and cruel (Saturn = Pluto) altercations (Mars = Ascendant). No positive influence can be expected from solar arc Mercury and solar arc Neptune transiting the com-plex of Moon's Node, Sun, and Jupiter.

Looking now at the sections from the wife's life diagrams we will also find factors and developments correlating with the terri-ble occurrence. The natal chart has a Venus-Saturn aspect and a progressed retrograde Saturn approaching Venus aspect that cor-responds to the pain of love and separation in love. The progressed Midheaven advanced to the critical position lines of Saturn and Mars, at the same time that the progressed Midheaven = Mars was almost exactly due. The mental confusion in this case is the result of progressed Mercury over Moon and Neptune (Figure 55).

The decisive factors among the solar arc directions were af-fected as well (Figure 51). The solar arc Midheaven contacted Ve-

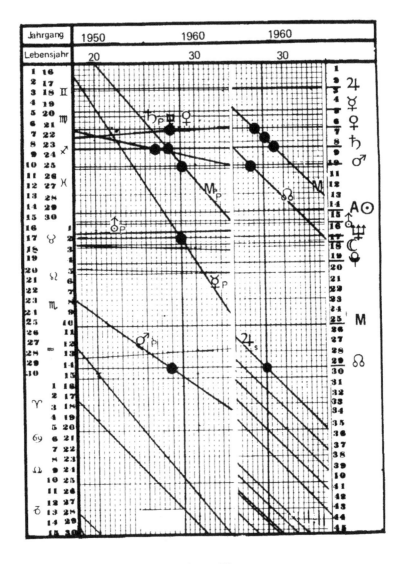

Figure 55
Section from wife's life diagram;
progressions; solar arc directions

nus and Saturn and the midpoint of Venus/Saturn. We must now also take into consideration that the natal charts have not been corrected, so that a slight shifting of the Midheaven is possible, making the constellation more precise. The explanation of solar arc Jupiter = Moon's Node can be found by considering Moon's Node at Venus/Saturn = Mercury/Mars. One might also be able to say that the wife, through death, was spared further years of torture in her marriage to a sick man.

The most significant directions have already been indicated in the natal charts of Figures 50 and 51, and these are solar arc Mars = solar arc Pluto and Saturn = Venus in the husband's case, and the solar arc Midheaven = Saturn in the wife's case. The main difference between these two methods of representation lies in the fact that the entry of the positions in a circle allows for only one year at a time (in some cases also the year previous to or following the year in question) to be grasped, whereas a larger period of time is covered by the life diagram, therefore facilitating preventive measures and planning for the future. When the diagrams of the couple in question are placed one over the other, the mutual due dates of directions become readily recognizable. Of prime importance are the corresponding times of all three methods: annual diagram, life diagram with progressions, and solar arc directions.

Husband and Neurotic Wife

Looking at each of the two cosmograms separately, the impression at first glance is a good one. Jupiter = Venus/Mars in the husband's case is normally indicative of a happy love life. The prospects for a good marital life are present with the wife as well in the form of Venus at the culmination point and Jupiter between Sun and Venus, or Jupiter at Venus/Pluto. In addition, we find the male Venus combined with the female Sun = Jupiter/Pluto. Seemingly, the only dubious factor is the opposition of Mars and Neptune in the wife's cosmogram. Each cosmogram should first be examined on its own and the cosmic state of the individual factors determined. This is done by turning the calculating disc to point to each

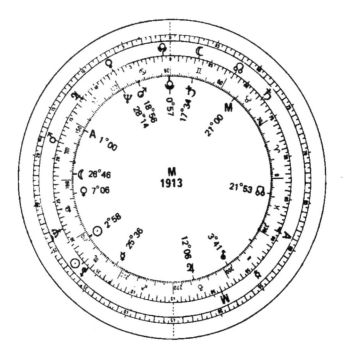

Figure 56

of the points in question in the 90° circle and then checking to see what aspects or midpoints result in turn. The following was determined in the husband's cosmogram:

SO = UR = MA/MC = ME/JU = VE/AS = *SA/DR*
MO = PL/DR = *VE/SA* = *ME/NE*
ME = AS/MC = *SO/SA* = *SA/UR* = *NE/DR* = MA/PL = VE/JU
VE = JU/PL = MO/MA = *SA/NE* = ME/MC
MA = JU/NE = *VE/NE* = S*A*/MC
JU = VE/MA = *MO/NE* = AS/MC
SA = *SO* = *UR* = *SO/NE* = *UR/NE* = PL/AS = *JU/MC*
UR = SO as above
NE=*VE/MC* = *ME/PL* = *MO/AS*

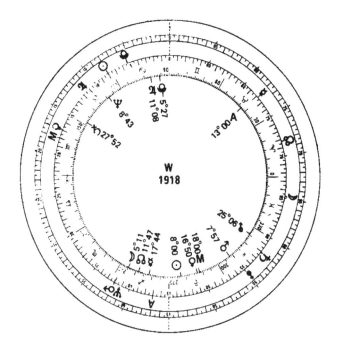

Figure 57

PL = MO/VE = JU/DR = *SO/AS* = *UR/AS*
DR = VE/PL = JU/PL = MA/DR
MC = VE/PL = JU/PL = MA/DR
AS = SO/PL = *UR/PL* = *VE/NE* = MA/JU

The negative configurations are in italics. And here we see that the prospects for a happy marital life are practically nil. Our object now is to determine in what way the positive and negative combinations coincide with those in the wife's cosmogram and to what extent these may be jointly triggered.

Let us now examine the wife's structural picture in the same way:

SO = JU/PL = MO/AS

MO = *SA/DR* = ME/UR = MA/PL = MA/NE
ME = *SO/SA* = JU/UR
VE = MC = ME/AS = MO/UR = *MO/SA*
MA = *NE* = PL/DR = MO/JU = *SA/MC* = *VE/SA*
JU = *SA/UR* = DR/AS = VE/PL = SO/VE
SA = *DR/AS* = *SO/MC* = *SO/VE* = *VE/PL*
UR = SO/JU = *VE/PL* = *NE/DR* = MA/DR = MO/AS
NE = MA as above
PL = *SA/AS*
DR = MO/ME = JU/AS = VE/MA = *VE/NE* = *NE/MC* = MA/MC
MC = VE = MO/SA
AS = SO/ME = JU/DR = MO/MC

The predominate configurations in the female cosmogram are those involving Moon, Venus and Mars.

Let us now look at the contact cosmogram. Venus = Sun and Pluto (1) and opposition Midheaven at (2) indicates a very strong bond, whereby only Venus = Saturn/Neptune in the male cosmogram and MC = Venus = Moon/Saturn in the female cosmogram have to be taken into consideration. These show up an abnormal tendency in the love relationship. The coinciding of the Jupiter positions (3) could be evaluated as positive if it were not for the participation of the husband's Moon/Neptune and the wife's Saturn/Uranus. Opposite we find Mercury = Uranus (4) alongside of Saturn. Here, too, the very negative midpoints have to be included. In the husband's case these are Mercury = Moon/Saturn = Saturn/Uranus = Neptune/Moon's Node, and with the wife these are Uranus = Venus/Pluto = Neptune/Moon's Node. The striking fact here is that the midpoint Neptune/Moon's Node is present in both instances. We find typifying for the wife's case the combination Uranus = Neptune/Moon's Node, indicating her unwillingness to accommodate to marital life. Mars = Midheaven = Venus (5) would result in a very strong or passionate relationship if the husband's Mars = Venus/Neptune did not indicate a lack of

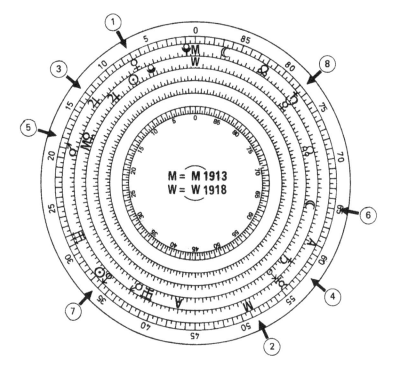

Figure 58

satisfaction and the wife's Midheaven = Moon/Saturn = Venus did not point to disappointment, renunciation, and isolation. Also coming into the picture is her Moon (6), which at Mars/Neptune = Saturn/Moon's Node indicates feelings of inferiority, sensitivity, weak nerves, woman's illness, alienation and isolation. Finally, we find Sun = his Uranus (7) = his Saturn = her Mercury (8), also expressive of a certain degree of rejection.

The main object in consulting the life diagram (Figures 59 and 60) consists in determining where correspondences among the various positions (entered in the graduated scale) are to be found and where progressive constellations have developed. This couple got married in 1943. Very clear-cut marriage constellations developed for both individuals. The husband has due progressed Venus = Pluto = Moon/Venus, progressed Sun = Mars = Jupiter/Neptune = Venus/Neptune = Saturn/Midheaven. The marriage is indicated in the wife's case by Jupiter = Sun = Jupiter/Pluto = Moon/Ascendant, and by progressed Mars = Jupiter.

Note the complex of Uranus, Jupiter, Saturn (3/4) present with the wife. Progressed retrograde Saturn first contacted Jupiter and then approached the natal Uranus. Progressed Uranus gradually approached natal Saturn. Around the year 1959, the progressed Midheaven contacted Saturn, thereby initiating the stimulation of progressed Uranus = Saturn. Progressed Saturn approached Uranus, and in the period 1965-1967, the progressed Sun contacted the critical constellations.

Special attention should be paid to the rule set up by the author and which has been repeatedly substantiated: A heavenly body is effective for the duration of time it takes it to travel one degree. According to the 1918-19 ephemeris, Saturn needs 14 days to cover this distance, and 14 days = 14 years. In this same period Uranus takes 16 days = 16 years.

The year 1959 saw a beginning state of emotional confusion and unrest. A physician sketched her condition with the following words: "Fear of life, severe inferiority complex, self-glorification, exaggerated arrogance and self-confidence, the unwillingness to grant others their own rights, fluctuation between love and hate even in relationship with her own husband, application of a truly superior intelligence towards solely negative ends."

Her admission to a mental hospital was only prevented by homoeopathic treatment in 1967. Her normal weight was around 102 pounds, and then for years she only weighed 88 pounds and was unable to gain any weight. This meant a disorder of the involuntary nervous system. Her last meal of the day was always at noon, and she did without any more food until seven o'clock the next morning. The abdominal organs were all in a very weak state, her

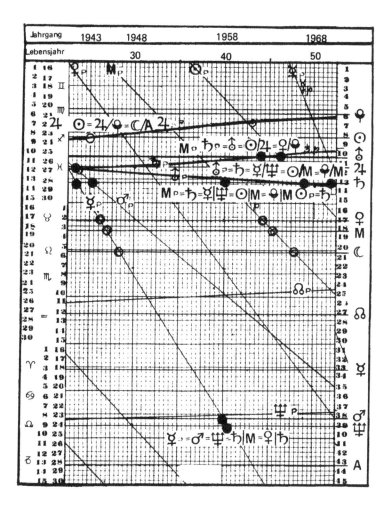

Figure 59; section from wife's life diagram; progressions

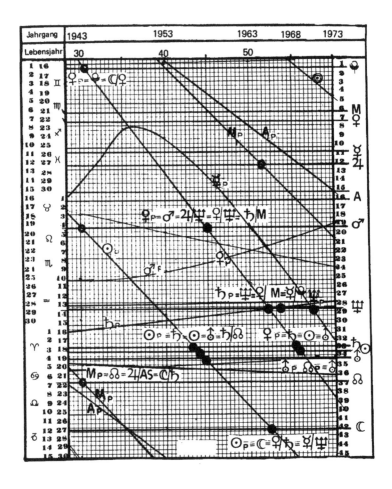

Figure 60; section from husband's life diagram; progressions

circulation poor. "Her attitude toward children is negative and rejecting, she has no interest in anything erotic, or sexual, be they expressed in words, pictures, or actions, magazine articles in this direction are overlooked. Unfortunately, her response to others does not exceed the superficial conventionalities. Her standpoint as to the existence of any such problems, and they do exist, is that she will just have to make do somehow." In spite of all this, her husband did not leave her, since he was indebted to her in other respects.

As of 1962, the wife carried on a correspondence with a man overseas. Altogether, their correspondence ran to approximately 2,500 typewritten pages up until his death in 1966. These were "unique love letters," which as the years went by contained more and more evidence of a fantasy divorced from reality. (Please note the transits of the progressed Midheaven over Venus, Midheaven and Moon from 1962 to 1966.) The husband wrote that the last two years, and especially the beginning of 1967, were terrible for him.

Only a few constellations with the corresponding statements from *The Combination of Stellar Influences* need be quoted here in substantiation of the foregoing information:

Progressed Saturn = Uranus: Inhibitions of rhythm, kicking against tutelage, the tendency to cause unrest in one's environment.

= Sun/Jupiter: The expectation of good luck, the disinclination to do anything, incapability and incompetence, inhibitions (partly conditioned organically), lack of success, illness.

= Venus/Pluto: Unusual experiences in love, tragic love.

= Neptune/Moon's Node: Inability to become an integrated unit of a community, emotional inhibitions with regard to partner.

= Mars/Moon's Node: Sudden unions and associations, reverse, inhibitions with regard to others, difficulties or disadvantages through unions and associations.

= Moon/Ascendant: Excitability, restlessness, inhibitions, depressed state, union with others through joint or common suffering.

Progressed Uranus = Saturn: The reversal of progressed Saturn = Uranus with the meaning remaining the same.

= Mercury/Ascendant: Sudden associations, mutual unhappiness, isolation.

= Sun/Midheaven: Psychological tension, inner conflicts, a negative outlook on life, reserve and withdrawal.

= Sun/Venus: Self-will in love relationship, sexual inhibitions, suffering in love, love-sickness.

= Venus/Pluto: Excitement and upset, a decision made in haste, the desire to bring harm to others, the inclination to harm oneself by exaggerating.

= Mercury/Neptune: A suddenly stepped-up power of imagination, ideas, misguided imagination, convulsive disturbances in connection with the nervous system, dark thoughts, pessimistic outlook on life.

On looking at the husband's life diagram we find indications of the crisis pending for the year 1959 expressed in progressed Venus = Mars = Jupiter/Neptune = Venus/Neptune = Saturn/Midheaven and in progressed Sun over Saturn, Sun, Uranus.

Here, too, a protracted direction is involved. Progressed Saturn approached Neptune = Venus/Midheaven = Mercury/Pluto, due around 1966 and intensified and triggered by progressed Venus over Neptune and later over Saturn, Sun, Uranus.

Referring to the contact cosmogram, we see that the reciprocal relationships at (3/4) and (7/8) in particular have been stimulated because of the protracted directions due here. At this juncture we unfortunately have to omit the consideration of solar arcs and the transits, since in such a case as this an entire book could be written on all the possible interrelationships and their stimulation and resolution.

Relationship with Girlfriend

In August 1971 I received from the husband of the previously mentioned neurotic wife a report based on the above facts relating his further experiences. The husband first furnished information on himself: "Admission to the hospital on April 13, 1970, partial resection on the bladder on May 14, 1970, the elimination of a malady of 30 years' duration. I had always had a urinal retention of 500 to 700 cc. In addition to this, Is underwent a prostatectomy (removal of the enlarged prostate gland)." In the cosmogram, the Sun is located at just under 3 Scorpio. In the book on the anatomical correspondences of the degrees of the zodiac reference is made under 3 Scorpio specifically to the prostate. As we may see from the life diagram, progressed Venus reaches the complex of Saturn-Sun-Uranus in the period 1968-1970 and thereby triggers the illness.

"On July 20, 1970, I went to a health resort for recuperation and on the very first day met the one and only woman for me, my life's companion if I had not already been married. (This corresponds to progressed Venus = Uranus in the life diagram, i.e., sudden love.) In October and Christmas of 1970 as well as Easter of 1971, this woman was a guest at our home. At first she was heartily welcomed by my wife, but then a continual alternation between invitation and cancellation began, until the relationship broke off entirely between her and my wife. I have been continuing the relationship secretly and have also spent a three week's vacation with this woman.

"My wife now only weighs 85 pounds, and her physical and emotional state is steadily deteriorating. As my doctor expresses it: 'She is being consumed by an inner blaze.' She is continually subject to a more or less great anxiety about the future which at

Figure 61

times borders on schizophrenia. When in such a state, she doesn't know what she is saying or doing. She calls other people a pack of liars and crooks who are pursuing and tormenting her. She herself states she is not suitable for this world and no longer lives in it.

"And now to my acquaintance. Here is a rather odd story. She first attended a school of commerce, but then interrupted her studies there and entered a Catholic order on August 27, 1956. There, she first worked in bookkeeping, then in the secretary's office, and underwent training as a nursery school teacher as the order required her to. On August 21, 1968, at 9:30 p.m., she escaped out the back door. On December 12, 1967, she attempted committing suicide by taking an overdose of tablets. She just barely escaped a serious mishap on a train on August 16, 1970, at 1:38 p.m., by being pulled back through the door of the compartment just on time."

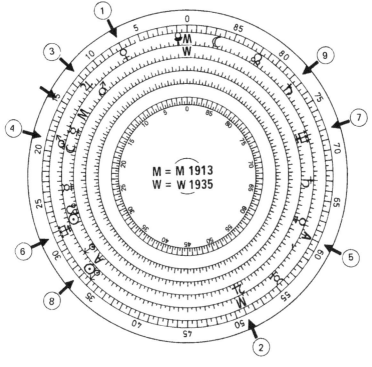

Figure 62

The following constellations developed in the woman's radix:

SO = DR = UR/PL = *NE*
MO = PL/MC = SO/MA = *VE/SA*
ME = MO/MC = MA/PL = VE = JU/NE
VE = ME = JU/NE = MO/MC = *MA/PL*
MA = VE/JU
JU = UR/NE
SA = VE/NE = *MA/UR* = *SO/MC* = ME/PL
UR = MA/JU
PL = SO/MO = ME/UR = AS/MC = *VE/NE*
AS = JU/MC

91

Again, there are several negative constellations present here affecting the love life, but there are also some positive aspects, and if we take a look at the contact cosmogram, we find evidence of strong ties.

On the basis of his Venus = his Midheaven = Jupiter at (½) a strong love can develop that due to his Jupiter = her Mars (3) could possibly lead to marriage.

At (4/5) his Mars = his Ascendant = Venus is just as powerful as the contact at (1/2). However, (6/7) his Neptune = her Sun = Neptune is very negative in value and could result in disappointment or a long-lasting mutual yearning because fulfillment is at first impossible

Aspects of separation are represented by his Sun = his Uranus = his Saturn = her Ascendant at (8/9). Nevertheless, the total picture given by this synastry must be regarded as positive. Although the age difference is considerable, it can be compensated by the great store of experience each of these partners has.

One Family's Haemic Disorders

The wife was born May 23, 1925, shortly after the New Moon. Unfortunately, the time of birth is unknown. Pluto = Sun/Neptune immediately strikes the eye in the natal chart at hand, and this very same configuration will also turn up in the cosmogram of the child.

The husband was born October 30, 1923. Again we have no birth time, but luckily the reverse is true in the child's case. Peculiar significance becomes attached to this couple's coming together through the comparison of the two cosmograms in the contact picture. It is certainly rare for two people joined in marriage to have been born on the same day and in the same place as is the case with this couple.

The contact cosmogram has at (1) the Mars positions in the 90° circle, and this is actually a square. In the case of the husband we

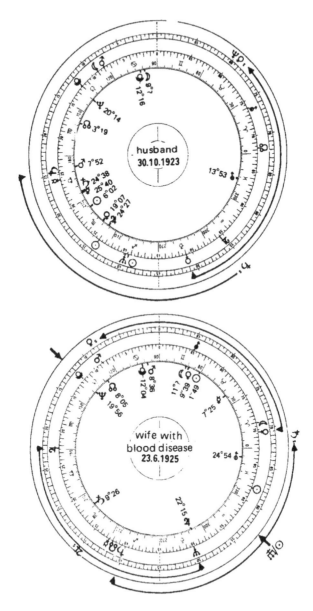

Figures 63 and 64

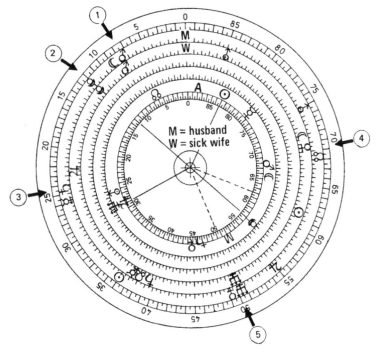

Figure 65

find Mars = Jupiter/Neptune, and we may presume Jupiter/Neptune to indicate bad (Neptune) blood (Jupiter). At (2) the Pluto positions coincide. However, this means that the mutual Pluto is located at the female midpoint of Sun/Neptune, and as the child's positions marked on the inside indicate, his Pluto is likewise located at this position at the midpoint of Sun/Neptune. The mother's constellation of illness is therefore also inherited by the child. At (3), the father's Saturn is located opposite the mother's Venus (4). Since Saturn is to be found at his Sun/Pluto and at her Mercury/Pluto, we may assume that the love relationship was in some way affected deleteriously. At (5) we find the third contact of mutual planets after Mars and Pluto, i.e., the contact between the two Neptune positions in the form of his Neptune = his Venus and

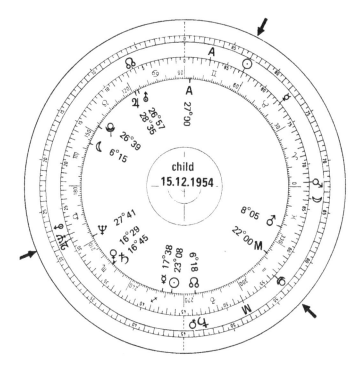

Figure 66

her Neptune = Sun/Saturn. This portends disappointment (Neptune) in love (Venus) for the husband due to an illness (Neptune = Sun/Saturn) of the wife.

The transcription of the wife's natal positions to the graphic ephemeris indicated that the child was most likely conceived as transiting Pluto and transiting Venus crossed over the mutual Mars (1). The consequences of this constellation quickly came to the fore. In April 1954, transiting Neptune passed over the mother's Venus and the father's Saturn. Likewise, transiting Mars contacted the Neptune positions (5) and transiting Jupiter contacted the mother's Saturn and Uranus. She suffered severe hemorrhage and loss of appetite, and she received intravenous injections of table salt and vitamin solutions "to adjust the body to the conditions of pregnancy." In October, at the beginning of the eighth month, the expectant mother had to be operated on for appendicitis. As early as September, Neptune, as at the time of conception, was transiting her Venus and his Saturn (3/4). In October, Saturn transited Saturn and Uranus, and several Mars transits became due at the same time. Transiting Pluto gradually approached the mutual Pluto position and at the moment of birth was located at Sun/ Neptune, just as Mars over Jupiter fell due—a familiar birth constellation.

In the child's natal chart shown in Figure 66, Pluto = Sun/Neptune can be clearly and indisputably recognized as a configuration of heredity. While Venus and Saturn are sesquiquadrate in the cosmograms of the husband and wife, these two planets form a close conjunction in the child's natal chart. The Midheaven in the child's cosmogram coincides almost precisely with the Neptune positions of the parents.

As to the child's development, in the first two years of his life he vomited daily, and sometimes even at every meal. He contracted measles at the age of eighteen months, mumps at five years of age, chicken pox at six, and in the late summer of 1960 the child's legs were covered with blotches of varying sizes. The aftermath of the chicken pox saw the child gradually deteriorate (solar arc Venus and Saturn = Midheaven = Saturn/Pluto = Venus/Pluto). Weekly blood transfusions became necessary, but he could not be saved.

To conclude this discussion we now shall consider the mother's life diagram. The progressions for the period of pregnancy and the birth show that progressed Mercury = Neptune = Sun/Saturn, progressed Venus = Sun = Venus/Neptune = Saturn/Uranus = Mars/Jupiter, progressed Saturn = Moon's Node = Venus/Mars. Among the solar arc directions we find the characteristic solar arc Venus = Mars (conception, birth), Moon's Node = Jupiter (mutual joy over the birth of the child), solar arc Mars = Mercury (excitement and upset).

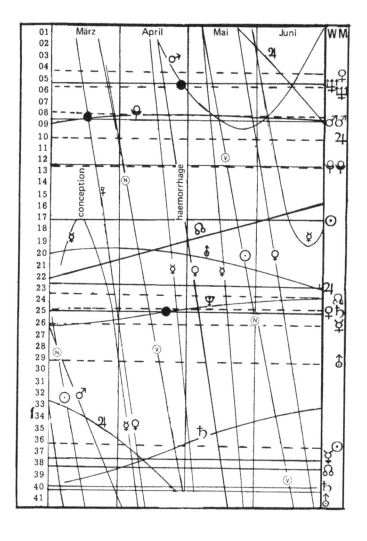

Figure 67

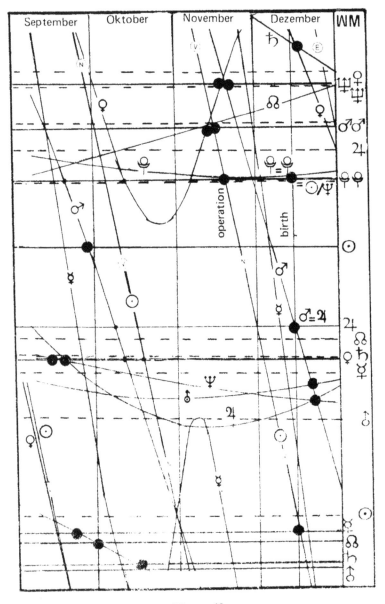

Figure 68

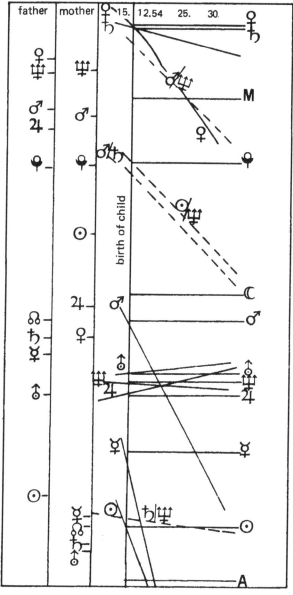

Figure 69

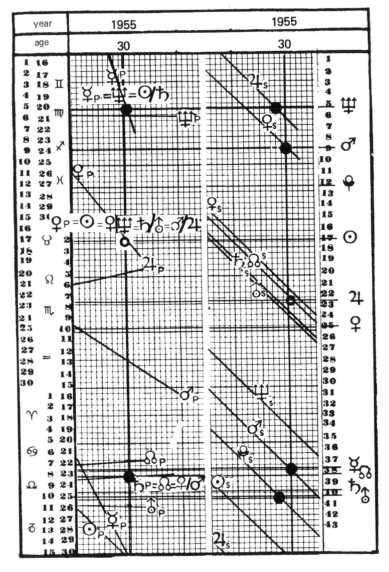

*Figure 70; section from wife's life diagram;
progressions; solar arc directions*

100

This example, therefore, demonstrates how most of the constellations in the contact cosmogram are triggered and resolved so that it should be possible in other cases to predetermine the periods when the contact constellations will become acute.

Sick Parents and Sick Children

The aspects of this case are of particular significance for a marital relationship since they demonstrate that even though abundant indications and tendencies are contained in the contact cosmogram, only a thorough investigation of each partner's cosmogram effectively throws light on the mutual relationship. Birth data:

Father: January 21, 1908, 10:45 a.m., 47N47, 13E03
Mother: August 14, 1912, 12:30 a.m., 47N47, 13E03
First boy: February 15, 1939, 8:10 p.m, 47N47, 13E03
Second boy: April 13, 1946, 7:30 p.m, 47N47, 13E03

The father had polio as a boy, and the result was a clubfoot on the left side. His appearance and posture is reminiscent of a Neanderthal man with his stocky build; highly set, broad shoulders; long and dangling arms; muscles more soft than pronounced; deep-set eyes; receding forehead, small nose; and thin lips. He is not unintelligent and is very personable. He is a very capable master craftsman.

The mother has a wide, low forehead; long, muscular extremities; and is slightly pigeon-toed. She is mentally sharp. The first boy also has these characteristics, along with expressive blue Aquarian eyes. He is mentally active and is a good student. The second boy is a typical Aries child, knows how to get his own way with stubbornness and perseverance, and is a little tyrant. He is deeply attached to his mother, and his face is finely-cut and sweet in expression. He has large, expressive eyes and a wide forehead.

Looking at this couple's contact cosmogram we find several critical contacts. Deep mutual affection does seem to be the result of his Venus and Moon with her Venus at (1), but which is nega-

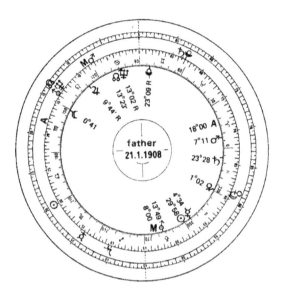

Figure 71

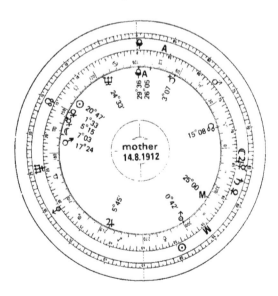

Figure 72

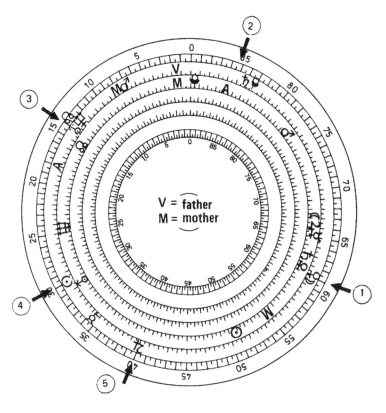

Figure 73

tively affected by her Venus aspecting her Saturn. Opposite at (3), the complex of Uranus, Neptune, Moon's Node m coincides with her Moon's Node. At (2), very difficult circumstances result from his Saturn and Pluto with her Ascendant and, opposite at (5), with his Jupiter. Finally, his Sun and her Uranus are conjunct at (4), whereby unexpected incidents should be anticipated.

The structural pictures, which should always be calculated for each partner, give us the first real insight into the difficulties and problems that have arisen for this couple. The cosmic states of Neptune are particularly striking. The wife has Neptune = Sun/

Pluto = Mars/Saturn and the husband Neptune = Sun/Pluto = Sun/ Saturn. According to *The Combination of Stellar Influences*, these mean, among other things, "Inhibitions in physical or mental development, undermining of health."

We know the husband had polio when he was four to five years old. We easily determine in the father's cosmogram in the 90o circle that solar arc Midheaven and solar arc Mars reached Neptune approximately in his fifth year of life, causing the above mentioned configuration to be triggered at the same time.

In the mother's case, Pluto s reached Neptune when she was around age twenty-five, thereby triggering the configuration given above. At the age of about twenty-six (1938), when the first son was conceived, solar arc Neptune was conjunct the Sun, which was located at Mars/Neptune. There was therefore reason to believe that a severe crisis was in the offing.

Continuing our comparison of the structural pictures we find the mother has Pluto = Saturn/Neptune = Jupiter/Neptune = Moon/ Neptune, and the father has Pluto = Moon/Neptune = Moon/Uranus = Venus/Neptune.

Furthermore, the mother's cosmogram contains Moon's Node = Sun/Saturn = Saturn/Midheaven, and the father's has Moon's Node = Sun/Saturn = Sun/Pluto. It is strange that very often persons with the same kind of disposition are attracted to one another and marry, thereby enhancing the severity of the negative tendencies. Further survey of the structural pictures shows us further configurations imperiling especially the health of both partners.

The very difficult birth on February 15, 1939 necessitated a blood transfusion. As the above elaboration tells us, it was just at this age that the mother was under the influence of the critical directions. After the birth of her first child she received a blood transfusion every day for a week because of the Rhesus (Rh) factor. About this, Ernst Pressecker, a Vienna surgeon, wrote:

104

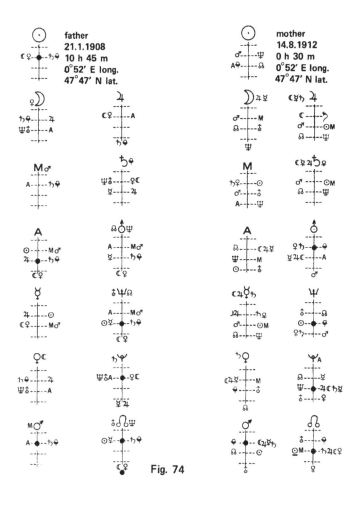

Fig. 74

105

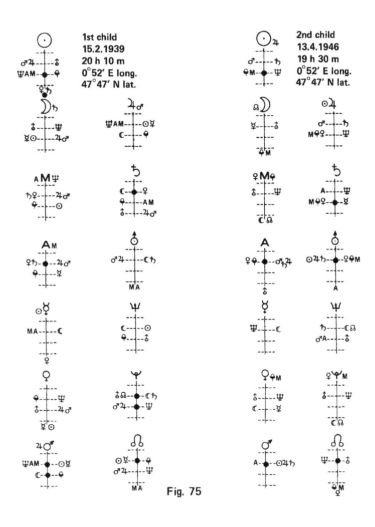

Fig. 75

Figure 75

106

"From the modern standpoint, no attributes of mind or character are transmitted from donor to recipient via a blood transfusion; the blood does nevertheless sometimes contain in addition to essential elements substances which can lead to serious harm in the recipient or even to his death. The discovery of the blood groups has effectively reduced the dangers of blood transfusions to a minimum. However, it has become evident that severe shock and blood decomposition still may result from a blood transfusion. Is n this, the determination of the so-called Rhesus factor was of significance (Rh). This is a blood characteristic primarily linked with the red blood corpuscles and which can make a blood transfusion dangerous. Of special importance and interest for the obstetrician is that the non-correspondence of these factors between mother and child can impair the blood-building organs of the embryo to such a degree that permanent damage can result for the child. We may assume that an infant's blood disease can be traced to the Rhesus factor. Foreknowledge of the blood group and the Rhesus factor can do much to prevent damage, nevertheless, limits should be set to the use of blood transfusions for women patients especially.

"During a second pregnancy, the mother's antibody count is increased. This may already have caused damage to this child or mean harm to the next. We are of the opinion that the blood diseases of the newborn are due to the Rhesus factor. The newborn's jaundice, especially of those prematurely born, can gradually develop into a severe decomposition of the blood involving changes in the conditions of liver, spleen and bone marrow."

At the time of the second boy's birth, the mother was subject to a triggering of the same constellation. By advancing the Sun thirty-four degrees, corresponding to an age of thirty-four years, we find the solar arc Midheaven entering a square to Pluto = Saturn/Neptune = Moon/Neptune and Jupiter/Neptune. This not only indicates disease but bad blood through Jupiter/Neptune.

The boy became jaundiced immediately after birth. After three months of normal development, the first disorders began to appear, which in his sixth month showed serious effects under Sun opposition Sun and resulted in rickets. In October 1947, at the age of eighteen months, the boy was admitted to the hospital because of general weakness and apparent anemia. There, decomposition of the red blood corpuscles was determined. The child's condition—his mental reaction and ability were good—was improved by the administration of medication and a special diet to the extent that he was able to walk better and more surely, although he remained unable to run like other children. Every October sees a return of his disorder. The child has no appetite and is tired and wan. He recovers in the spring.

The comparison of the children's structural pictures with those of the parents produces a great number of correlations, Sun, Neptune and Pluto again being prominent among these.

The first boy has Sun = Neptune/Pluto = Midheaven/Pluto = Mars/Uranus. The second boy has Sun = Neptune/Pluto = Midheaven/Pluto = Mars/Saturn.

The first boy has Mars = Sun/Ascendant = Sun/Neptune = Moon/Pluto. The second boy has Mars = Sun/Ascendant = Saturn/Ascendant. In addition, there are a number of disease constellations not shared by both of the boys.

Similar correlations can be seen in the two children and their parents. In the case of the mother and the first child, Mars = Moon/Pluto, Saturn = Moon/Venus, Pluto = Jupiter/Neptune coincide. These correlations are present between the mother and the second child: Saturn = Venus/Mercury, Uranus = Saturn/Pluto.

We find the following similar midpoints shared by the father and the first child: Sun = Venus/Saturn, Ascendant = Jupiter/Saturn, Pluto = Moon/Uranus, Moon's Node = Sun/Pluto. Between the father and second child we find the following correlations: Ascendant = Jupiter/Pluto, Mars = Saturn/Ascendant, Moon's Node = Uranus/Neptune.

We may conclude from these correlations that the blood transfusion given at the birth of the first child was not solely responsible for the illness of the second child, but rather the astronomic hereditary factors also played a significant role.

For this reason young couples intending to marry should absolutely make it a point not only to consider the contact cosmogram but also to compare structural pictures. Certain illness tendencies will be present, but by no means should the same ones be held in common by both. This would lead to an intensification—as in this case—of the correlating planetary pictures.

A Child: Compelling Grounds for a Marriage?

A young man, somewhat over thirty years old and as yet unmarried, is looking for a wife, particularly since he would very much like to have children. However, he is very strongly tied to his mother, whose Sun and Moon aspect his Jupiter. As long as a strong link to the mother still exists and the mother still takes constant care of the son, there is only a slight chance of his ever marrying since he has not yet learned to make his own independent decisions. A psychological problem such as this should also be brought into consideration in marriage counseling.

He met a woman and fell in love with her, and their relationship has had consequences. The woman was very set on getting married and gave up her job. However, although he was to have a child from her, his doubts about the advisability of their marrying increased. What should he do? Should he marry the mother of his as yet unborn child, taking the risk that they may not be suited to one another and the marriage turn out to be very disharmonious, or would it be better for them to separate while there was still time?

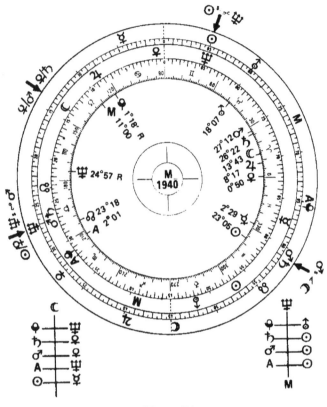

Figure 76

The counselor may be in a position to examine the problem, but he can in no way make the decision for those seeking his advice.

As it turns out, the young man preferred separation and will now have to pay child support. In the meantime, he has found a new girlfriend.

In the male's case, a very massive occupation of the sign of Aries is evident, so that he will try to assert his own will. Due to Mars conjunction Saturn, he will have to overcome many obstacles in order to do so. His relations with women are most likely peculiar and very difficult, for we notice when looking at the lunar structural picture a striking contradiction in that on the one hand Moon is located at Venus/Mars, thereby indicating a strong urge for partnership and union, and on the other hand the Moon at Venus/Saturn may result in lack of satisfaction, dislike, and separation. Moon at Neptune/Pluto can correspond to a peculiar emotional life, Moon at Neptune/Ascendant can lead to a lessening of good relations and to disappointment, and Moon at Sun/Mercury most likely indicates a very emotionally accentuated relationship, but this constellation is more or less swamped by the other negative tendencies present here.

The aspect of Mars and Saturn also engenders contradictions. Whereas Mars at Sun/Venus leads to physical love, Saturn brings about separation. The structural picture of Neptune at Uranus/Pluto = Sun/Saturn = Sun/Mars = Uranus/Ascendant = Neptune is also extremely negative in character.

Around 1971-72, the solar arc Sun approached the opposition to Neptune so that in this period there was danger of disappointment. Although solar arc Mars semisquare Moon = Venus/Mars makes conception possible, the subsequent Saturn brings about a separation. Solar arc Jupiter enters a favorable aspect to Jupiter but at the same time a negative one to Neptune. Finally, solar arc Neptune aspects Mars and Sun/Venus, a further indication of disappointment in love.

Let us now consider the girlfriend's natal chart. Immediately evident is the Sun-Neptune-Saturn aspect, making an abnormal disposition possible. On the one hand, we find the Midheaven conjunct Mars, pointing to a certain degree of willpower to shape one's own destiny, but on the other, the Midheaven is located at Neptune/Ascendant, and this signifies: "The misfortune to suffer from lack of resistance and stamina or from lack of self-control . . . the tendency to act under the influence of others, also to lay oneself open to being led astray or corrupted by others." This combination was later confirmed.

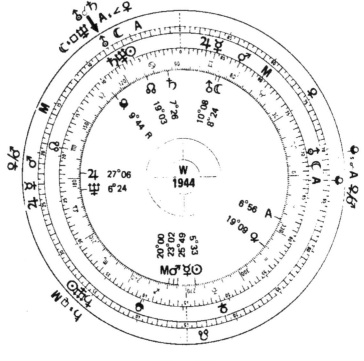

Figure 77

A consideration of the directions in the outer 90o circle shows us that solar arc Pluto entering the opposition to the Ascendant at Venus/Mars is significant. This indicates great passion, sexual union, and accordingly, conception was a possibility in this year. Solar arc Moon reached the square to Neptune, corresponding to a disappointment (Neptune) for a woman (Moon).

Solar arc Saturn sesquisquare the Midheaven can be interpreted to mean severe strain. Solar arc Uranus conjunct Saturn indicates great emotional tension and quarrels, which indeed turned out to be the case with this couple. The solar arc Ascendant semisquare Venus = Midheaven/Moon's Node points to love and sexual relationship.

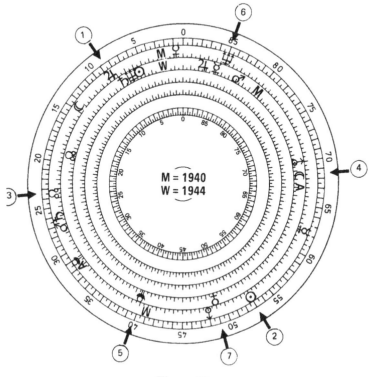

Figure 78

The contact cosmogram contains a great variety of combinations. At (1/2), difficulties and drawbacks are indicated by his Jupiter = her Sun = her Saturn. At (3/4), his Moon's Node = her Moon = her Uranus/Ascendant corresponds to a sudden emotional contact. At (5/6), his Midheaven = her Pluto relates to an inevitable or fateful relationship that, because his Neptune = her Mercury, results in disappointment. His Uranus = Venus at (7) means love at first sight, but only of short duration.

Presented here is a section from the annual diagrams for the period around the date of conception, November 28, 1971. Annual diagrams placed alongside of each other represent at the same time a contact cosmogram. This makes possible the simultaneous deter-

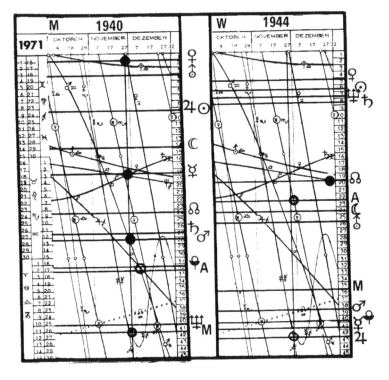

Figure 79

mination of to what degree the same configurations are due for both individuals and in which cases only one of the persons in question is affected. One advantage of the 45° system in this connection is that the semisquare and sesquisquare aspects do not have to be searched for; rather, they appear in succession along with the others. For example, in this case we immediately find his Uranus = her Venus, his Jupiter and Sun = her Saturn and Neptune, his Moon's Node = her Moon, etc.

The greater activity of the man is recognizable for the date of conception. Venus and Pluto jointly transited the Venus position, sufficing to excite passion to an unusual degree. Jupiter and Mars approached Pluto and Ascendant, and Venus and Mercury transited the Midheaven. The transits of Saturn, Uranus, and Neptune over Mercury already give hints of unpleasant consequences. Mars to Mars = Sun/Venus is very characteristic. And here the Neptune direction is also stimulated.

It seems odd that the constellations in the female annual diagram are not as strong or effective. Of significance here is the transit of Mercury and Venus over Jupiter, whereas the Midheaven is located at this position in the male cosmogram. Transiting Sun over the Ascendant simultaneously triggered the solar arc Pluto. We see from all this how important it is to include the directions in all our considerations.

Lesbian Love

The first woman was born March 17,1892, 11:50 p.m, 150E, 53N (Figure 80). This woman was always regarded as being "mannish." She preferred masculine attire, had a masculine haircut, and spoke with a deep, manly voice. Her figure was described as being "sturdy." She had a limp due to a chronically inflamed knee-joint; the cartilage was almost completely destroyed. She lived with the woman introduced below for many years, was the head of a men's haberdashery, and owned a villa. As of 1950, she broke off her relationship with the other woman.

The second was born August 7, 1888, 2:45 p.m, 14E34, 53N25 (Figure 81). This very feminine woman lived with the woman above for many years and took care of her household. She had been married before. Since both husband and wife had not taken their marital vows very seriously, they were divorced. Afterwards, she had a few short-lived affairs until she moved in with her partner.

She was of average height, "pleasantly plump," had light blond hair and blue eyes, and was said to have been very pretty in her younger days. She was very chatty, but suffered occasionally from depression, and she tried several times to take her own life and liked "playing with death."

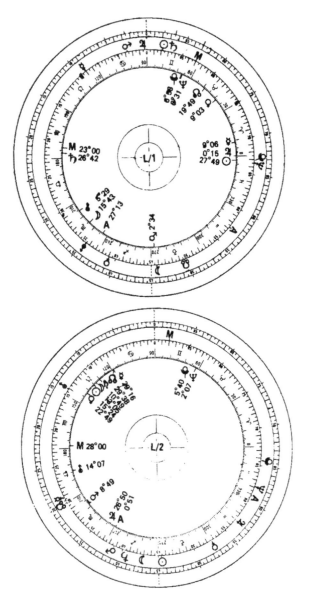

Figure 81

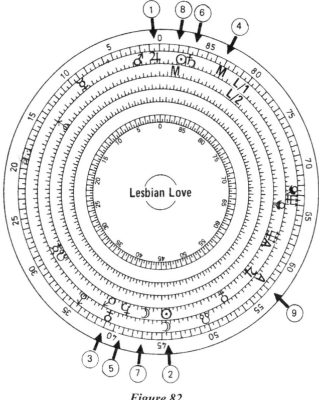

Figure 82

If this was indeed a lesbian relationship, then the contact cosmogram would have to show some combinations like those to be found with married couples.

And this is the case. At (1) and (2) we find in the case of the first female's Jupiter = Moon = Sun/Mars, which indicates the optimistic husband. Also at (2) we find the second woman's Sun = Venus/Mars, indicating the urge for physical love and the union of man and woman.

The personal attraction through the Midheaven (4) = the first woman's Venus = the second woman's Mars can assume a passionate character. Saturn = Saturn at (5/6) signals a separation at a later date. Ascendant = Jupiter at (9) typifies a good mutual relationship.

The break-up of the relationship in 1950 becomes understandable when we notice that in that year Pluto transited 15-16 Leo and thereby the contact point Moon = Sun (2). Here, Pluto led to the separation of the women.

Chapter Five

Collaborators

Krupp and Beitz

In 1953, Alfred Krupp, owner of the Krupp works, became acquainted with Berthold Beitz at the home of an artist living in West Germany. Beitz was at that time the general director of an insurance company, but in November 1953, he became chief representative of the Krupp company. He worked out a new organizational structure and set new guidelines for the company's policy. At that time, the corporation encompassed ninety-seven individual companies and its annual volume was more than four billion marks.

The success combinations in Beitz's cosmogram are easily determined. We find them concentrated in the upper left region of the 90o circle, namely Jupiter = Mercury/Mars, Mars = Sun/Jupiter, Sun = Mars/Pluto, Mars = Mercury/Pluto, Mercury square Jupiter, Sun square Pluto, Mars opposition Jupiter.

From his fortieth year of life on (1953), these constellations began to act as directional triggers, affecting, among others, solar arc Mars sesquisquare Pluto, solar arc Jupiter sesquisquare Sun, solar arc Mercury ses- quisquare Mars. In the contact cosmogram, these success configurations coincided with the complex of Mars-Moon-Uranus (1) = Pluto/Moon's Node (business concern).

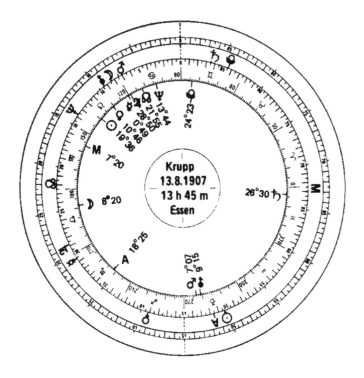

Figure 83

At the same time, the Mars positions (3) and Krupp's Moon coincided with Beitz's Jupiter (1). This joint constellation was also triggered by transiting Pluto (opposite).

Influential in the association of the industrialist and the company's representative was Pluto = Sun/Mercury (5) = Krupp's Sun/Jupiter and Beitz's Moon's Node (5). This combination was triggered by transiting Jupiter in 1953.

This same constellation played another role, however, when the corporation was in the midst of a crisis and had to ask for federal support in March 1967. In contrast to the consolidation of this constellation in 1953 through the transiting Pluto, Neptune, the great

120

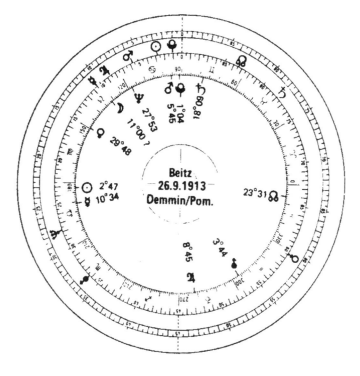

Figure 84

dampener of success, had now come to the force, while at the same time transiting Saturn on the opposite side approached the connecting complexes. This crisis may also have led to Krupp's timely deadly on July 31, 1967, partly because he, as sole owner of the corporation, found its conversion to a stock corporation irreconcilable with his viewpoint.

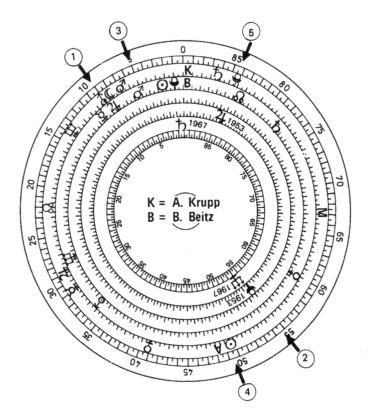

Figure 85

122

Herrligkoffer, Buhl, and Ertl

In the year 1953, the German Nanga Parbat expedition was started Karl Herrligkoffer (H), physician and natural scientist, who was born June 13, 1916, 8:35 a.m. CET, Schweinfurt, West Germany. He was the half-brother of the mountain climber Willi Merkl, who died in 1936 while climbing Nanga Parbat. After learning about the planned expedition, Herrligkoffer decided he had to be a participant.

Despite the fact that he had no Himalyan experience behind him and was not a well-known alpinist, he was appointed the head of the expedition and was able to collect sufficient funds through grants to support the German-Austrian plan.

Herrligkoffer also managed to engage the talented and well known mountaineer Hermann Buhl (B) to take part in the expedition. Buhl was born September 21, 1924, 3:45 a.m., Innsbruck, and he succeeded in making a solo climb to the peak of Nanga Parbat on July 3, 1953.

The cameraman for the expedition was Hans Ertl (E), who was born February 21, 1908, in Munich. Ertl had already been a participant of many expeditions before, such as the 1932 Greenland expedition, climbing four peaks over 7,000 meters, and also the Chilean expedition 1938-39.

As long as they shared a common goal, the three mountaineers worked together in harmony, but after their goal had been achieved, the relationship among the trio was beset with difficulties. The relationship between Herrligkoffer and Buhl was especially strained, giving rise to a belittling of Buhl's performance and to widely differing judgements of his personality. Herrligkoffer also clashed with the cameraman Ertl, a conflict that later landed in court and which was not resolved until 1954.

Looking at each of the three cosmograms separately we first notice the presence of a strong aspect between Neptune and

Figure 86

Moon's Node in each natal chart; in Herrligkoffer's and Buhl's we find a conjunction, and in Ertl's case an opposition. This configuration is indicative of a lack of communal spirit, of a difficult adjustment to teamwork, and also of disappointment due to false expectations. These closely linked Neptune-Moon's Node combinations are again to be found in the contact cosmogram, in that Herrligkoffer's aspect is located at the midpoint of the other two.

Only one joint axis of success is present. At (1) and (2) Jupiter aspects Mercury (H) = Mars (E) = Mercury and Jupiter (8), and this axis is triggered by the transiting Jupiter at the time of their achieving their goal.

Close by we see a very unfavorable configuration (3/4) in the form of Neptune, Moon's Node (H) = Saturn (B) = Mercury (E).

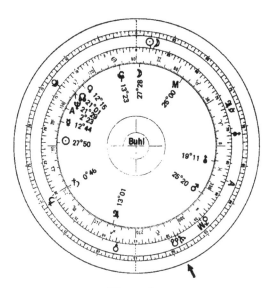

Figure 87

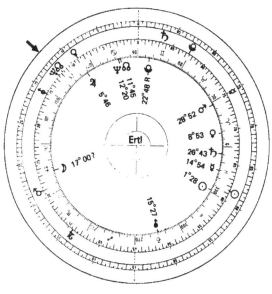

Figure 88

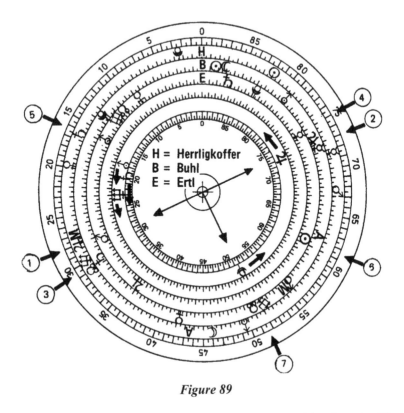

Figure 89

First Jupiter and then Saturn also joined this combination. At (5) we find a combination negatively affecting teamwork, namely Saturn (H) = Uranus (E) = Ascendant (B) = Sun (E), which can result in difficulties and upset. At (7), Pluto was located at a right angle to the axis of success, but this success was somewhat diminished for Buhl at the first because of the location of Moon's Node and Neptune at this point in his natal chart.

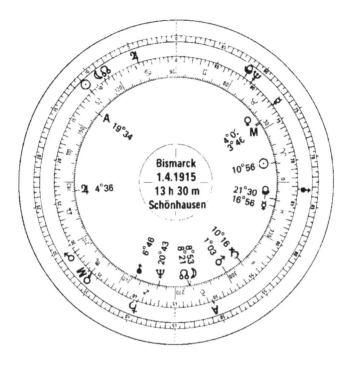

Figure 90

Wilhelm II and Bismarck

Due to the great age difference, genuine understanding or good collaboration could hardly be expected to exist between the young Emperor Wilhelm II, who began his reign at age twenty-nine, and Bismarck, the Iron Chancellor and founder of the German Reich, who was seventy-five at the time.

With the Sun square Pluto, the young ruler had the absolute desire to assert his authority and power. He remained unaware of the fact that this was in direct contrast to his capabilities. Please note Sun at Saturn/Pluto and opposite Neptune = Mars/Midheaven. In the contact cosmogram, the Pluto positions are located directly opposite to each other, forming a very unfavorable mutual aspect.

Figure 91

Wilhelm's Midheaven coincides with Bismarck's Pluto and Neptune (4), and opposite we find Wilhelm's Pluto aspecting the Chancellor's Venus and Midheaven (1/2). Close by, (3/4), the Emperor's Neptune and Sun are in opposition. At (5), the Pluto positions coincide with one another opposite Wilhelm's Mars/Neptune. Unusual excitement is indicated by the Emperor's Ascendant (7) opposite the Chancellor's Uranus (6). This constellation was triggered by transiting Mars and the gradually approaching Pluto, just when Bismarck, on the Emperor's urging, had to resign his position on March 20, 1890. A high government official, Hollstein, then succeeded in blocking the renewal of the reciprocal assurance agreement with Russia, although Russia with the consent of Bismarck had expressly wished the prolongation of the agreement. It was an irrevocable mistake.

128

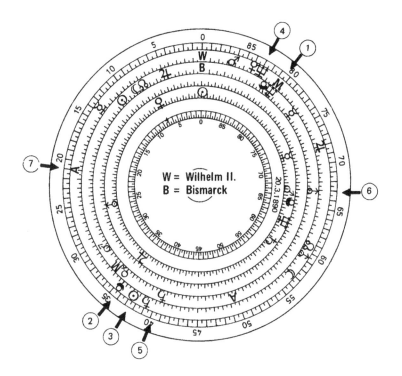

Figure 92

Adolf Hitler
20.4.1989
18 h 30 m
Braunau/Inn

Figure 93

Hitler and Goebbels

A great deal of Adolf Hitler's success would have been un-
thinkable without the work of his collaborator of many years'
standing, Josef Goebbels, who was later Hitler's minister of propaganda. Hitler's popularity is marked in the cosmogram by Moon
conjunction Jupiter, but which when located at the midpoint of
Mars/Neptune had to result in the fooling of the people. At the
same point (3), we find Goebbels' Midheaven at Mercury/Pluto,
while Mercury and Pluto themselves are sesquiquadrate to one another. This indicates a convincing orator who is capable of
strongly influencing the masses. However, this constellation is
also located at Mars/Saturn, on the death axis, leading us to the
conviction that Goebbels, by means of his mass influence, brought

Figure 94

death and destruction to the multitude. We remember all the soldiers who fell in battle, the mass extermination of the Jews, and the prisoners tortured to death in the concentration camps.

Goebbels also had Moon and Jupiter aspected, and these bodies were located at the midpoints of Mercury/Uranus, Moon's Node/ Uranus and Uranus/Ascendant. Accordingly, he was able to assess every situation correctly and to influence others to his own advantage or to achieve his own ends, and could be sure of great persuasive powers (1). This constellation is now aspected with Hitler's Mars, which, located at Mercury/Pluto and Pluto/Ascendant, makes one inclined to criticize, makes one convinced of one's ability to master great tasks, instils the desire to avoid no risks or dangers, and makes one capable of great compelling power.

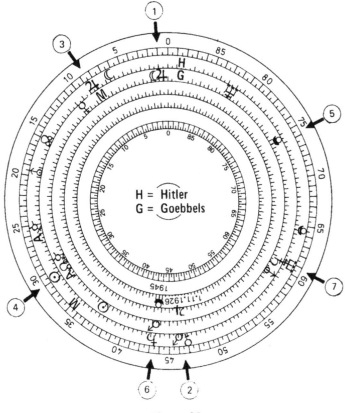

Figure 95

The joint struggle for power in the state is best reflected in Hitler's (4) Sun and Goebbels' (5) Pluto opposite. This position is intensified in Hitler's case through Sun = Ascendant/Midheaven = Mercury/Midheaven and in Goebbels' case through Moon's Node = Mercury/Ascendant. In contrast, however, the conjunction of Hitler's Saturn and Goebbels' Mars (6) as well as Neptune and Saturn (7) must be regarded as extremely critical. The various constellations were subsequently triggered, but for the purposes of this discussion, closer attention should be paid to two significant events: As Goebbels became the gauleiter of Berlin on November

132

1, 1926, he reorganized the party structure and found an effective mouthpiece in the newspaper *Der Angriff* (The Attack). He also took over control of the party propaganda. On Goebbels assuming his duties, transiting Jupiter was aspecting the constellations at (1/2). During this period, solar arc Moon = solar arc Jupiter = radix Mercury = radix Moon's Node = radix Ascendant in Goebbels' case, and solar arc Jupiter = Mars = Mercury/Pluto in Hitler's case became active.

Very characteristic at the time of their simultaneous deaths was the transit of Pluto over Hitler's Saturn and Goebbels' Mars in that Pluto = Mars/Saturn corresponds with a violent death.

Hitler and Goerdeler

The former mayor of Leipzig, Karl Goerdeler, was appointed to the position of Reich commission for the supervision of prices by Reich President Hindenburg on December 8, 1931, and after 1933, was also consulted by Hitler on administrative questions. On November 5, 1934 he was reestablished in his position dealing with price controls. His vehement opposition to Hitler first became evident when, in direct contradiction to his orders, the Mendelsohn monument in Leipzig was removed and never replaced. With great determination, he resigned from his position, and many Germans recognized him as a courageous man who would not kowtow even to the dictator Hitler. He then became the head of a resistance group that planned the assassination attempt against Hitler on July 20, 1944. If the assassination had been carried out successfully, Goerdeler was to have become chancellor of the Reich; however, the assassination attempt was a failure. Goerdeler fled, but after several weeks of aimless and desperate wandering, he was discovered by an air force aide and arrested at the end of August 1944. On September 9, 1944, he was sentenced to death and executed on February 2, 1945, in Plotzensee.

In contrast to the Hitler-Goebbels relationship, we must assume that completely different correlations are in effect here. In the con-

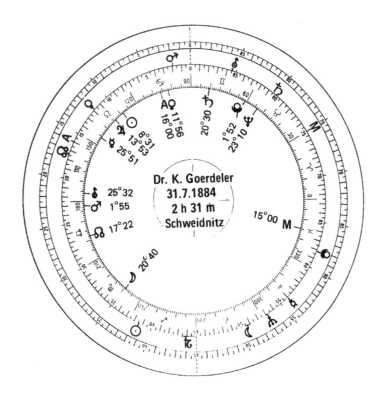

Figure 96

tact cosmogram, the Mars positions directly oppose one another (½). Of interest here is the fact that Mars in both cases is located at Sun/Neptune, so that in any event misguided (Sun/Neptune) energy (Mars) would have been probable. Goerdeler chose assassination as a means to an end. Hitler was opposed by an extremely capable and competent personality. The fact that the transiting Neptune was located on this mutual Mars at the time of the assassination attempt is characteristic. Almost all of the other mutual aspects are negative. Moon's Node = Ascendant (3) would be favorable for collaboration, if Neptune = Pluto (4) were not located opposite, undermining teamwork and cooperation. Hitler's Uranus = Pluto (5/6) was triggered by the transiting Mars at the time of the

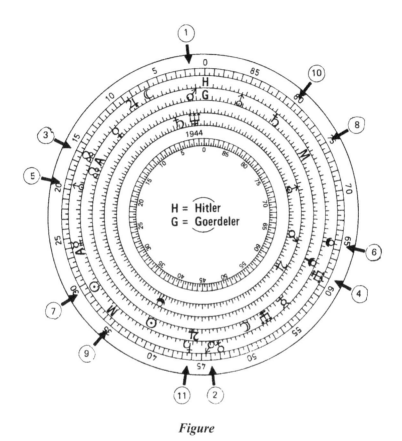

Figure

assassination and corresponded to a sudden injury. Sun (7) = MC (8) could also be considered positive. However, Midheaven (9) = Saturn (10) had to make any cooperation difficult. Saturn = Jupiter (11) negatively affected their mutual relationship.

Chapter Six

The Contact Cosmogram in Daily Life

The many examples Is have presented in this book should amply demonstrate to what degree the contact cosmogram gives a true reflection of the relationship between two individuals.

1. The contact cosmogram provides an objective basis for the assessment of the mutual relationship of two or more persons. After all, one person's contact with another can be based on any number of reasons, e.g., attractive appearance, a striking personality, unusual charm, physical charm, a great show of tact, great vitality", etc. But it is just this sort of personal attributes that hinder any kind of objective view of an individual.

2. A person can change. Even the just-married shows himself in a completely different light. What outward appearances had concealed are now revealed. In the course of time, too, the individual and his relations with others also undergo changes. It is therefore necessary to relate the contact cosmogram with the current stellar positions in order to determine in the first place which factors were instrumental in bringing about mutual attraction or liking. Was it merely a cursory acquaintanceship, triggered only by a Sun, Mars or Venus transit? Did Uranus stimulate a relationship which is per-

haps but short-lived? Was an unusually passionate relationship brought into life by a Pluto-Venus aspect? Did Jupiter give his blessing to a stable and continuing relationship? As a rule, only part of the mutual cosmic contact points are triggered at the time of the first meeting. The question then arises as to what happens when the other aspects come into effect.

3. There is a difference between examining the contact cosmogram of lovers, of fiances, married couples, or collaborators. In the first instance, the main role will be played by those stellar bodies influencing love, i.e., the aspects involving Sun, Moon, Venus, Mars, Jupiter. Collaboration in the fields of business or science will mean the consideration of combinations among Mercury, Sun, Mars, Jupiter, and Moon's Node. Midheaven and Ascendant will in any case play a significant role, providing the birth time is known and these personal factors can be computed.

4. The contact cosmogram enables us to acquire deep insight into the relationship between two different individuals. Yet it does not tell us all. The contact cosmogram and a handwriting analysis are sufficient groundwork for an examination of the relationship between immediate superior and subordinate, to use one example, in order to set up a personal affidavit. If, however, it concerns a leading figure in the company who is to assume directive or managerial duties for many years to come, then more extensive investigations are just as indispensable as in a marriage prognosis.

5. A thorough investigation of both natal charts of a couple planning to marry is necessary for the contact cosmogram. Of special significance is a comparison of the structural pictures. Very helpful, too, is the setting up and comparison of cosmopsychograms for the two individuals involved. The life diagrams drawn up on the basis of the solar arc directions and progressions can inform us as to the course of events to be encountered in their married life. The life diagrams should be annually supplemented by the annual diagrams, in order to determine the positive and negative periods and take conscious measures to face these correspond-

ingly. In fact, it is the contact cosmogram we need to inform us in each case when directions or transits will be passing over the contact points or whether it will merely be a matter of transits taking place in the individual cosmogram.

6. We should always be aware of the fact that we are able to examine and assess only the cosmic factor. However, there are many things involved which lie beyond this. Considerable age difference, contrasting milieu and upbringing, great differences in the level of education, differing viewpoints on life or religious confessions, heredity, racial difference, differences in financial status, etc. may—but do not necessarily have to—be decisive in the formation and further development of a relationship. Many differences and difficulties can be overcome by awareness and a consistent way of life; the essential point here, however, is that not just one but both partners are willing to shape their lives accordingly.

A quote from Friedrich Schiller's poem, "Die Glocke" (The Bell):

Drum prufe, wer sich ewig bindet,
ob sich das Herz zum Herzen findet.
Der Wahn ist kurz, die Reu' ist lang.

Roughly translated:

Be sure thy bond for all eternity
rests on true affinity;
the madness is short,
the regrets everlasting.

7. There is no reason to assume that the contact cosmogram is only of interest to young people intending marriage. Rather, the contact cosmogram can also be of aid in clarifying a relationship in later years, after the initial period of infatuation has passed, and even when thoughts of separation have arisen. Daily practice has shown in just such situations as these that the contact cosmogram,

along with the total analysis of the individual by means of cosmogram and cosmopsychogram, is of particular value in achieving a basis for mutual understanding. Many a marriage on the point of breaking up has been mended in this way.

Here is yet more proof that it is cosmobiology's mission to provide help for modern-day man, for there is no other branch of science capable of comprehending in this same way the entirety of an individual and, simultaneously, the time factor. With the contact cosmogram there is an additional aspect to be considered, i.e., that of a couple being seen as a unit. It therefore can contribute in some measure to developing the duality of many couples into a truly harmonious unity.

Explanation of Abbreviations

MC	Midheaven
AS	Ascendant
SO	Sun
MO	Moon
ME	Mercury
VE	Venus
MA	Mars
JU	Jupiter
SA	Saturn
UR	Uranus
NE	Neptune
PL	Pluto
DR	(Dragon's Head) Moon's Node
V	Full Moon (in the graphic ephemerides)
N	New Moon (entered in the solar orbit)

The birth data in the cosmograms is given in the German manner: 8.12. means December 8, 11.5 means May 11.

Lightning Source UK Ltd.
Milton Keynes UK
UKHW011127031121
393318UK00001B/339